WASHINGTON:
Christians
in the
Corridors
of Power

WASHINGTON:
Christians in the Corridors of Power

James C. Hefley and Edward E. Plowman

TYNDALE HOUSE PUBLISHERS, INC.
Wheaton, Illinois
COVERDALE HOUSE PUBLISHERS, LTD.
London, England

Library of Congress Catalog Card Number 75-13635. ISBN 8423-7815-4, paper. Copyright © 1975 by Tyndale House Publishers, Inc., Wheaton, Illinois 60187. All rights reserved. First printing, July 1975. Printed in the United States of America.

*To all the ambassadors of Jesus Christ
assigned to Washington, D. C.*

Introduction

Two days before Gerald Rudolph Ford assumed the presidency of the United States, amid the debris of Watergate and the impending resignation of Richard Nixon, Ford slipped into the office of House Republican leader John Rhodes of Arizona. There he joined Rhodes, a Methodist, and Republican Albert Quie of Minnesota, a Lutheran and long-time friend, for a short prayer meeting. Although the times were such that even a crusty cynic wouldn't begrudge politicians grasping for the Almighty, the prayer meeting was not a desperate it-has-come-to-*that* session. Nor was it one of those press-bedecked rituals of religious patriotism that sometimes seem to accompany momentous occasions in national political life. The prayer group, which included a fourth member, former Secretary of Defense Melvin Laird, a Presbyterian, had been meeting for months. It was simply that day of the week again. (Episcopalian Ford, Quie, and Laird had first started praying together in 1967.)

The group, noted *Time* magazine, was but "one of an intricate web of groups and individuals—almost an underground network—stretching well across religious and political boundaries, all of them part of a small but growing spiritual renaissance in Washington."

Indeed, that web extends into much of official Washington. From the White House and Pentagon to Capitol Hill and the departments and agencies of government, the story is the

9

same: groups of individuals—blacks, whites, ethnics—are
meeting to pray, to discuss the Bible and moral implications
of their faith, to seek the spiritual solutions they believe
America needs, to tend each other's wounds. Some groups
are large (several dozen or so persons meeting at a time), most
of them are small. On the job, members of these groups may
differ on matters of policy-making and voting, but they are
committed to God and to each other, and this has led to a
mellowing—even easier-reached compromises—in the
political process.

Many of these groups have ties to a movement once known
as International Christian Leadership. Launched on the West
Coast in the thirties, it took root in Washington in 1941. The
annual National Prayer Breakfast, attracting nearly
everybody at leadership level in the executive, legislative, and
judicial branches of government, is but one of the outgrowths
of ICL's ministry. In an attempt to de-institutionalize ICL,
its leaders now refer to it simply as "the fellowship." An
important ministry center related to it is Fellowship House,
which hosts a few of the groups while spawning others.

Some groups have their origin in local churches. Some have
sprung up almost spontaneously, the result of Christian
believers discovering each other and finding that they have
mutual interests and concerns.

Moving quietly among these groups are persons who, while
eschewing the title, nevertheless function as full-time or
part-time missionaries and evangelists. Most of them are
laypersons. Some are staked by churches and friends, others
support themselves. Unlike the street preachers and religious
protesters who come and go, these resident workers hang in
there year after year, working for spiritual renewal at the
nerve-center of the nation. If it happens here, they reason, it
can change the country, maybe the world.

Spelled out in daily routine, their work may involve
counseling a congressional staffer whose marriage is going
sour, praying with a newly converted lawyer struggling to put
his affairs in ethical order, organizing a prayer breakfast
(they don't just happen), arranging a luncheon with a foreign
ambassador who's shown an interest in Christianity,

discussing with a Senator the spiritual issues implicit in an upcoming vote.

In the some eight months between the energy-crunch Christmas of 1973 and President Nixon's resignation, when the main headlines were occupied with Watergate and other crises, another story emerged: something involving God and man was happening in Washington. Ex-Nixon aide Charles Colson, a Teamsters lawyer and the reputed tough guy of the Watergate cast, had gotten converted and was talking—about Christ and changed values. His mentor in the faith, outspoken Iowa Democrat Harold Hughes, announced he was giving up his Senate seat at the end of his term in early 1975 to become a full-time Christian worker. Oregon Republican Mark Hatfield led the Senate to endorse a national day of prayer and humiliation, echoing a similar call by Abraham Lincoln in a time of national distress more than a century earlier. State and city officials across the land voiced their support.

There were other faith-related stories, interviews with Christian personalities, editorial musings on Ten-Commandment morality, all reaching a crescendo in saturation coverage of Gerald Ford's inaugural speech, essentially a religious one. As a result, tens of millions of Americans during this period of national melancholy were exposed to the claims and meaning of biblical Christianity.

At times, Washington's religious scene was—and still is—marked by debate. Some of it revolves around matters related to the constitutional wall of separation between church and state, and whether America is in danger of embracing a civil religion. Some of it pertains to issues of social justice and to what degree, if any, Christians should be involved or speak out—and on which side. Some of it concerns evangelist Billy Graham's role in national life; should he be less visible as a confidant of presidents and more outspoken as a prophet? Some of it is over priorities for Christian involvement in the face of exploding global needs. Some of it is basic: does being a follower of Christ make a difference in the way one votes on knotty issues?

With the variety of viewpoints and deeply ingrained

political differences that exist among the Washington
believers themselves, clear-cut "Christianization" of national
policy cannot be expected soon, if ever. Yet spiritually-rooted
changes *are* occurring among individuals in or close to
government, changes that hold potential national
significance. These developments constitute not a torrent of
revival, as United Press International's Wesley Pippert points
out, but "single droplets of water [wearing] away at the old
paths and ways of doing things."

In summary: Washington's mini "renaissance," to quote
Time, goes on.

This book is the story of that movement, the story of what
God has been doing in Washington lately.

CHAPTER ONE

Ford's Faith

A study of the spiritual mood of Washington can begin at the top, in the White House itself. For President Gerald Ford is a Christian, an acknowledged follower of Jesus Christ.

He is a faithful churchgoer. He meets periodically with several close friends for prayer, He reads the Bible daily. He gets frequent spiritual input from evangelist Billy Zeoli and from others, including son Michael, a divinity student at an evangelical seminary. He alludes on occasion to his trust in Christ. His important speeches are laced with God references that ring true.

"There is nothing artificial about the President's public expressions of religion," affirms church-scene analyst Martin E. Marty, of the University of Chicago. Even sometimes skeptical journalists concur. "For him," says James Reston of the *New York Times,* "religion is not a role but a reality; he doesn't fake it but lives by it."

The so-what reaction of the secular mind aside, Ford's faith poses an enigma to a lot of his fellow Christians who, partly because of their own categorical identities, can't quite figure him out.

Many mainstream church leaders, while not doubting the sincerity of his faith, lament that he is not a "fully aware" Christian (translation: one committed to liberal socio-political policies). They cite his conservative voting record as a congressman, his presidential proposals calling for welfare cutbacks in the national budget, and the like.

Others, questioning his sense of justice, still have not forgiven him for pardoning Richard Nixon without first allowing the law to run its course. Some wonder why out of fairness he did not make similar concessions toward Nixon underlings convicted in the Watergate affair.

Among many fundamentalists and evangelicals like, say, the Baptists and Pentecostals, Ford's life style is an issue. He is a long-time member of the Episcopal Church, where moderation rather than abstinence is the watchword in matters of drink, and where "worldliness" does not necessarily include smoking and dancing—as preached for decades in evangelical circles. Ford often drinks a martini or two before dinner and cocktails at parties. He smokes a pipe. And he and his wife Betty dance at social gatherings.

Some church people don't care. What matters, they contend, is that the President is basically an honest man, a down-to-earth nice guy with decent ethics and a sense of dependence on the Almighty in trying to deal with the incredibly complex and explosive problems of our time. Still others dismiss a consideration of his faith and personality as totally irrelevant to a discussion of the presidency. They say the only important issue is whether he has the ability to carry out the demands of his office in these crucial times.

A large number of evangelicals are gun-shy about claiming Ford as a brother. They laid claim to President Nixon as one of their own (the boyhood conversion at an evangelistic crusade, the Graham connection, the White House services), but in the end they were embarrassed—and embittered—by what the Watergate tapes revealed about their man. "Let's not make the same mistake, presenting him as a born-again Christian without really knowing his true commitment," cautioned a conservative Christian congressman right after Ford became President. It is unlikely that the bulk of evangelical leaders will ever again be so unquestioning in their acceptance and support of a President. Ironically, this disenchantment with the White House occurs at a time when a theological kinsman occupies it.

Ford began his presidency the same way as all thirty-seven

presidents before him—his left hand on a Bible, his right hand uplifted as the oath of office was administered. The family Bible was held by his wife, Betty, and opened to the third chapter of *Proverbs,* verses five and six, Ford's favorite passage: "Trust in the Lord will all thine heart; and lean not unto thine own understanding. In all thy ways acknowledge him, and he shall direct thy paths."

(When he was sworn in as Vice-President it was over a copy of the Jerusalem Bible son Michael had purchased. It was opened to the first verse of Psalm 20: "May God answer you in the time of trouble.")

Repeating after Chief Justice Warren Burger, Ford affirmed, "I, Gerald R. Ford, do solemnly swear that I will faithfully execute the office of President of the United States and will do the best of my ability to preserve, protect, and defend the Constitution of the United States. So help me, God." He became the eleventh Episcopalian to invoke the help of God in the most important job in the world.*

In his inaugural speech that followed, Ford acknowledged the "extraordinary circumstances" under which he was assuming the presidency, "an hour of history that troubles our minds and hurts our hearts." He said he was acutely aware he hadn't been elected by ballot, "so I ask you to confirm me as your President with your prayers. And I hope that such prayers will also be the first of many."

Both his credo and compassion came through clearly in the memorable final portion of his speech. Excerpts:

> I believe that truth is the glue that holds government together, not only our government but civilization itself. That bond, though stained, is unbroken at home and abroad.
>
> In all my public and private acts as your President, I expect to follow my instincts of

---

*His ten predecessors: George Washington, James Madison, James Monroe, William Henry Harrison, John Tyler, James Polk, Zachary Taylor, Franklin Pierce, Chester A. Arthur, and Franklin D. Roosevelt. Not all were active church members, and Pierce became an Episcopalian after he left office. Six presidents were Presbyterians. Others: Methodists and Unitarians, three each; Baptist, Disciples of Christ, Dutch Reformed, and Quakers, two each; one Congregationalist; one Roman Catholic. Thomas Jefferson and Abraham Lincoln claimed no religious affiliation.

openness and candor with full confidence that honesty is always the best policy in the end.

My fellow Americans, our long national nightmare is over.

Our Constitution works; our great Republic is a government of laws and not of men. Here the people rule. But there is a higher power, by whatever name we honor Him, who ordains not only righteousness but love, not only justice but mercy.

As we bind up the internal wounds of Watergate, more painful and more poisonous than those of foreign wars, let us restore the Golden Rule to our political process, and let brotherly love purge our hearts of suspicion and hate.

In the beginning I asked you to pray for me. Before closing I again ask your prayers for Richard Nixon and for his family. May our former President, who brought peace to millions, find it for himself. May God bless and comfort his wonderful wife and daughters, whose love and loyalty will forever be a shining legacy to all who bear the lonely burdens of the White House.

I can only guess at those burdens, although I have witnessed at close hand the tragedies that befell three Presidents and the lesser trials of others.

I now solemnly reaffirm my promise ... to do what is right as God gives me to see the right, and to do the very best I can for America.

God helping me, I will not let you down.

Across the nation people were deeply moved. Much of the bitterness and anguish over Watergate and the impeachment crisis dissipated overnight. There was no cynical post-speech sniping by the television commentators and little by the syndicated columnists. NBC-TV anchorman John Chancellor ended his news commentary with the request, "Let's all say a prayer for our country."

"What we have agonized over in prayer has finally happened," remarked Iowa's Harold Hughes, who was giving up his Senate seat to engage in full-time lay ministry in the capital. "The faith of the people will now be rapidly restored."

An atmosphere of euphoria settled across the land following that inaugural speech on August 9, 1974. But a month later, on a Sunday morning at that, it was swept away by the storms of protest over Ford's pardon of Nixon.

The honeymoon with the electorate was over.

The President was born Leslie Lynch King on July 14, 1913, in Omaha, the son of a wool dealer. Two years later his parents, Leslie and Dorothy King, were divorced. Mrs. King, who had graduated from an Episcopal girl's high school in Chicago, returned with her son the next year to her parents' home in Grand Rapids, Michigan. In her early twenties at the time, she caught the eye of paint salesman Gerald R. Ford at an Episcopal church social. They were later married, and Ford adopted the boy, renaming him after himself.

Attendance at Sunday school and church services was part of the family's life. The elder Ford was an usher and an officer at Grace Episcopal Church, and Dorothy was active in women's work. He was also involved in local Republican politics, but the family's community life centered around the church. Religion was not talked about very much at home, yet it permeated the family's relationships, observes Thomas Ford, one of the President's brothers.

Young "Jerry" joined the Boy Scouts and rose to Eagle Scout ranking in a troop sponsored by a Methodist church near his home. At South High School in Grand Rapids, he starred as a center in football.

Jerry one day sought out Father Donald Carey, Grace's rector, and requested baptism. Because of the circumstances surrounding his early home life, he'd missed being baptized as an infant, the customary practice in the Episcopal denomination. The request was not born of deep spiritual trauma; the youth apparently considered it simply a step necessary to complete his own personal ties to the church.

Carey, recalling the occasion to reporter Hiley Ward, said

he told the boy: "Jerry, the Lord isn't going to love you any more before or after you are baptized." The pastor wanted to make sure Ford's mind was on more than just the ritual itself.

Ford went on to the University of Michigan, where he turned in a B performance in most classes and did better on the gridiron. As center, he was named the team's outstanding player of 1934, a bad year—seven losses, one win. His football experiences, he believes, helped him "many times to face a tough situation in World War II or, in the rough-and-tumble of politics, to take action and make every effort despite adverse odds."

After graduation in 1935, he turned down offers to play professional football. He chose instead to coach football and boxing at Yale. On the side he took law courses, eventually graduating from Yale Law School in 1941. During his days at Yale, he got involved briefly with a New York modeling agency through a Powers model he was dating. This landed him on the pages of *Look* and *Cosmopolitan*, modeling sportswear.

Throughout his college and law-school days, religion apparently was not an important surface factor in his life, though undoubtedly it functioned as a deeply embedded guidance system in ethical matters.

In 1941 Ford went back home to Grand Rapids and joined a law partnership. Then came Pearl Harbor. He joined the Navy and served for nearly four years, part of it in combat as an officer aboard the aircraft carrier U.S.S. *Monterey* in the South Pacific. On leave one day he came to Rector Carey and asked how to conduct a funeral. He feared that someday he would have to conduct a burial at sea.

"All you have to do is read it from the prayer book," said Carey. "It's pretty hard to botch up the Book of Common Prayer."

"Is it okay to say the Lord's Prayer in the burial rite?" Ford asked.

"You can say the Lord's Prayer anywhere," replied Carey.

The war over, Ford resumed law practice in Grand Rapids, taking time to teach Sunday school at Grace. Only now he had a hankering to run for Congress. Prospects seemed bleak: He

was an Episcopalian without a Dutch name in a
predominantly Dutch district (Grand Rapids is headquarters
for the Dutch-oriented Reformed Church in America and the
Christian Reformed Church). But the times were right, and at
age 35 he defeated the Republican incumbent in the 1948
primary, going on to win the election with a solid majority—as
he also did in twelve subsequent elections. He maintained his
membership at Grace over his years as a congressman but was
able to attend only occasionally.

One of Ford's campaign workers in the 1948 election was
divorcee Elizabeth Bloomer Warren, a department store
fashion coordinator and a former professional dancer with
the Martha Graham troupe. The pair were wed quietly three
weeks before the election and managed to squeeze in a two-day
honeymoon between political rallies. Afterward, they moved
to the Washington area, where they've lived ever since.

In 1955 they moved into a four-bedroom house they built
in the Virginia suburb of Alexandria. They became active as
"communicants" (though not "members") in Immanuel
Church-on-the-Hill, an Episcopal church on the grounds of
the historic Episcopal seminary in Alexandria. Ford served as
a church usher, headed up a parish commission working to
achieve fair housing and to provide aid to low-income
families, helped to establish a Capitol Hill issues-discussion
group made up of parish members, and even preached on
occasion. He seldom missed a Sunday church service when he
was in town, says Michigan bishop H. Coleman McGehee,
who was Immanuel's rector from 1960 until 1971.

Betty at times taught Sunday school and helped out in
other programs. Because of Ford's long hours and many
weekends away from home, much of the upbringing of the
children—Michael (born in 1950), John (or Jack, 1952),
Steven (1956), and Susan (1957)—was left to her supervision.
She made sure church was part of everybody's weekly
agenda.

In Congress, the team-spirited Ford became a party
stalwart, racking up a fairly solid conservative voting record.
A workhorse, he spent a lot of time in the House chamber,
did his homework, and stayed abreast of his assignments on

key committees. Somehow he managed to spend a day or two almost every week in Grand Rapids, holding forth in his field office. His votes on legislation for the most part accurately reflected majority sentiment in his district and, under Republican administrations, presidential views. He voted against major social legislation advocated by Presidents Kennedy and Johnson, proposals on which church leaders across the land were split along conservative-liberal lines. His mixed record on civil rights and other social measures gained him the hostility of many black church leaders.

Not until 1967 did Ford personally encounter any organized church opposition to his stance. Having become minority leader of the House in an intraparty coup in 1965, he was leading opposition to the 1967 open-housing bill when a group of clergymen from Grand Rapids descended on his office and persuaded him to rethink his position. On top of this, two of his closest friends parted company with him over the issue: New York's Charles Goodell and Minnesota's Albert Quie (pronounced Kwee). So did respected evangelical ally John Anderson of Illinois. Another close friend, Wisconsin's Melvin Laird, stood by him, but Ford ended up voting for a modified version of the bill.

Ford attended rather regularly the Thursday prayer breakfast for House members, though less frequently after he became minority leader. In the late 1960s he began meeting with Presbyterian Laird and Lutheran Quie for brief sessions of prayer on Wednesday mornings.

One day in 1960 Ford was puttering around his field office in Grand Rapids when a tall, black-haired, nattily dressed man in his late twenties stopped by "to meet my congressman."

After a vigorous handshake he introduced himself as Billy Zeoli, an executive with Gospel Films, a Michigan-based firm specializing in the production and distribution of evangelistic motion pictures for young people.

The ensuing small talk got around to sports, a mutual interest.

"Something clicked," says Zeoli. "We became friends." Before leaving, Zeoli gave Ford a Bible.

There were more visits, the conversations moved from sports to spiritual matters, and soon Zeoli was meeting with Ford both in Grand Rapids and Washington for prayer and Bible study. These meetings continued monthly even after Ford took up residence at 1600 Pennsylvania Avenue in the capital. In between sessions, Zeoli sent a weekly memo entitled "God Has a Better Idea," containing a Bible verse and a prayer. An occasional phone call also kept them in touch.

Zeoli grew up in Philadelphia, the son of colorful evangelist Anthony Zeoli, an ex-con turned evangelist. Billy thought of going to Yale or Harvard to take up law or business, but his father suggested he take one year at a Bible college first. Billy entered Philadelphia Bible Institute (now Philadelphia College of Bible), and the one year became three. After that came Wheaton College in Illinois, where he graduated in 1955. He'd been ordained by an independent Presbyterian church, and his eyes were on youth ministry. He landed a job as director of Indianapolis Youth for Christ. On the side he preached at evangelistic rallies.

At age 28 he became vice president of Gospel Films, an affiliate of Youth for Christ. Later he was named president. Under his aggressive leadership the company developed into one of the world's largest distributors of religious films.

Two former athletes, Bobby Richardson of the New York Yankees and Bill Glass of the Cleveland Browns (now an evangelist himself), introduced Zeoli to pro sports. Zeoli became a favorite pre-game chapel speaker among professional players, both in baseball and football. The chapel sessions today are often held in locker rooms before a game, many times with the majority of a team's players in attendance.

It was at such a chapel meeting in 1971 that Ford reportedly underwent an experience of spiritual renewal. Zeoli was speaking to a group of Washington Redskins football players, and Ford had accompanied him. Afterward, Ford lingered behind for a period of spiritual introspection and meditation. Neither Zeoli nor Ford will talk about that or any other of Ford's private religious experiences, but to those present it seemed the chapel message and prayer had some sort of special impact upon Ford.

Zeoli's extroversion and moderately flamboyant ways frequently make for unfavorable first impressions. "He's an *evangelist?*" exclaimed a woman staffer at the White House after Zeoli strode by, talking to everybody in sight. To the woman, a member of a conservative suburban church, Zeoli's air and appearance did not match the "proper" image. Commented Grand Rapids businessman Russell Kniff to reporter Strober: "Billy looks and acts like what many conservative Christians think people should not look and act like. But God looks at people from the inside, and from this perspective Billy is in almost every respect what a Christian should be." (Zeoli, his wife, Marilyn, and their children attend the independent Calvary Church in Grand Rapids.)

Those who survive first impressions (not everyone has bad ones) find Zeoli to be sincere, serious about life despite all the wit and good humor, and genuinely concerned about the well-being of his friends. Pro athletes and others tell how his counseling and encouragement have helped them improve their attitudes, save their marriages, and get them past other rough spots spiritually.

It was true friendship and concern, not a bid for favor or press attention, that prompted Zeoli to fly to Washington in the wee hours to pray with Betty Ford and her family before dawn on the day of her cancer operation in September 1974.

"Billy helped us as a family to integrate and temper our emotions," Michael Ford told a reporter. "He provided great strength."

Mrs. Ford is quoted as saying: "Billy carries his church with him. He doesn't need a building to make you feel close to God; he finds his little sanctuary for Christ wherever he is. My children all adore him. He makes God feel human to the young. He's quite a man."

(Betty Ford, like many political wives, has had more than an ample share of fishbowl-life pressures, loneliness, and one-sided family responsibilities. A pinched nerve, incurred when she tried to open a stubborn window, added to her grief. Sometimes the pain and stress coincided. She used tranquilizers to get past the bad times, and occasionally she drank. At one point she consulted a psychiatrist. In the end it was the strengthening of her faith that got her out of the woods, to the place where even cancer could not damage her buoyancy of spirit. She sets aside a period of time each day for prayer and devotional reading.)

In the summer of 1973, Ford and Zeoli met at a Grand Rapids hotel for breakfast and Bible study. Afterward, Ford invited the evangelist to deliver the opening prayer at a session of the House. The date chosen was October 11. As it turned out, that was the day after Spiro Agnew resigned in disgrace as Vice President and the day before President Nixon nominated Ford as successor.

Ford was subjected to a closer scrutiny than any national candidate in the nation's history. Some 350 FBI agents rummaged through his past and present, checking out his friends, finances, and private dealings. Colleagues on Capitol Hill grilled him in grueling hearings against the backdrop of the Agnew scandal and the unraveling of Watergate. He came up Mr. Clean. Meanwhile, the confirmation ordeal apparently drew the Fords closer to each other and to God.

"It's been an uplifting experience," Michael Ford told a *Christianity Today* reporter. "We've all been drawn closer together and we're giving each other spiritual support through prayer. It's brought about a real revival of our dependence and trust in God. [The prospects] are so crucial, so demanding, that I know Dad is getting deeper into the faith."

His nomination confirmed, Ford took the oath of office on December 6, 1973, in the House chamber. In addition to whatever else it was, the vice presidency proved to be a period of spiritual preparation for the presidency. Although Ford traveled a lot, he was able to spend more weekends with his family at church. As the tribulations of Watergate deepened, he found himself reaching out more often to God, his prayer life becoming more intense. He prayed and discussed Scripture with Zeoli, Laird, and other close friends. His faith was reinforced by the witness of Michael whom everybody calls Mike.

Zeoli and Gospel Films in January 1974, sponsored in Grand Rapids a prayer luncheon at which Ford was honored. The Vice President spoke briefly to the 1,000 persons there. Reporters noted he omitted any mention of God or Christ in his speech, a point some fundamentalists referred to later in questioning the authenticity of his faith. After Ford sat down, Zeoli called on Mike to pronounce the benediction. The youth, a freshman at Gordon-Conwell seminary in Wenham, Massachusetts, preceded his prayer with a short account of how he came to faith in Christ. It happened in the summer of 1970 on Nantucket Island, Massachusetts, between his first and second year at Wake Forest University, a Baptist school in North Carolina. Explained Mike:

> I had gone up there to work with several friends of mine. It was my first summer of really being away from home, away from parental control, and away from my peers at school. I was on my own. I just kind of lived it up. I broke free and experienced true growing and learning.
>
> I came into contact with many young people from all across the nation. They had different ideas and thoughts about the important topics of this nation: politics, drugs, Viet Nam, and religion.
>
> It was during that time when I was exploring for myself and really living a life of fun, frolic, and personal satisfaction that I realized that all the joy and peace I was experiencing was very temporary. All of it was channeled to number one, to me, myself.
>
> I was leading a life where I was the center. Everything revolved around me. I looked at myself as a nice guy, someone who was easygoing, thoughtful, mannerly. Yet inside I realized that I cared about myself first. I was going through life, directly or indirectly, focusing everything back to myself.
>
> I was convicted about where my priorities should be. I thank God that some of my closest friends

shared the truth with me that Jesus Christ came down from God the Father in flesh. He walked on this earth. He was subjected to temptation, trial, and persecution, yet He lived the perfect life. He was completely righteous. He faithfully and obediently walked through His life toward the cross of Calvary to offer up Himself, to take our place, to take our sins upon Himself so that we may live eternally.

It was during that summer that, through the work of God's Spirit in my heart, I realized the new life available through Jesus Christ. I thank Him for how He's touched my life. In the three and a half years since then, I have gone through spiritual ups and downs, but God's love for me has remained constant.

Each of us is offered this wonderful gift of eternal life through His son, Jesus Christ.

At Wake Forest Mike majored in political science, intending to go on to law school. But by his senior year his outlook had changed. He felt "called" to a ministry among young people. This caused some surprise at home, he recalled later, "but Dad knew my Christian faith was playing a strong part in my decision." He said his father helped him investigate seminaries, warning him away from "liberal" schools and suggesting instead a seminary that held a "strong orthodox view of Christianity."

Not long after Mike gave his testimony at the 1974 Grand Rapids prayer luncheon, Ford at a House prayer breakfast told his friends his own faith was strengthened by the impact that faith in Christ had made on Mike's life. In an interview, former congressman John Dellenback of Oregon, who was at the breakfast with Ford, commented: "Normally, influence flows from parent to child. In this case it flowed the other way. Jerry and Betty were impressed by the way the Lord took a grip on Mike's life."

At a Capitol Hill prayer meeting shortly before his father became President, and with his father present, Mike prayed:

"Protect him and keep him strong in spirit.... Grant him the courage to trust in you always and not in the things of this world. Work in his heart [so that he will] seek your guidance and direction in all things."

Another spiritually impressive event for Ford was the wedding of his son to Gayle Brumbaugh in the spring of 1974. With Ford standing by Mike's side as best man, the couple exchanged marriage vows they had written themselves:

> I, Mike, choose you, Gayle, to be my wife united in Christ from this day forward. I commit myself to share with you the realness of life, recognizing both the brokenness and the beauty around us, to create with you a home in which the peace of God is known and the need of others is recognized, and to look to God's guidance in all that we do. I promise to seek an attitude of understanding and forgiveness, and offer my constant love to you, my life's companion, until my presence is required by Christ.

Gayle then repeated the same promises. Later, as they prepared to take up housekeeping, the couple requested Secret Service agents "who like to go to church."

Soon after the wedding the Supreme Court handed down its decision requiring President Nixon to give the Watergate tapes to the special prosecutor. It became apparent to many in the Administration that Nixon's days were numbered. Some of Ford's friends and aides began meeting secretly to plan for the transition. On August 7, two weeks after the court decision, Ford joined congressmen Quie and John Rhodes of Arizona for the group's weekly prayer meeting. Reporters who spotted them emerging from a room on Capitol Hill were incredulous when Ford explained he and his friends had been praying, not devising political strategy.

The next day, Thursday, Ford was summoned to the Oval Office in the White House at 11 A.M. Nixon, nodding, shook hands with him and remarked, "I know you'll do well." That night Nixon announced his resignation to the nation, and the following day at noon the presidency changed hands, marked by Ford's memorable, faith-accented inaugural talk.

Two days later, true to their normal Sunday routine, the Fords went to church. To Ford, it was no super-special occasion, but to his fellow-parishioners and the pastoral staff at Immanuel Church-on-the-Hill that particular Sunday was indeed special: the President of the United States had come to worship.

Ford, his wife Betty, and Susan sat on the last pew, feeling just a little self-conscious about all the hubbub surrounding their visit. Rector William L. Dols, Jr., preached on death and renewal. There is a season for everything, he said, even upheaval and death, but the main issue is "where we will go from now." His point was that the nation should not languish in self-pity, but should pull itself out of the grave of political disaster.

The greatest danger, warned Dols, is "to allow Richard Nixon to become a scapegoat for us, to believe that by sending him into the wilderness he will bear the guilt of us all and we will be free from blemish." Each must deal with his own guilt, "pick up the pieces," and make a new start, he exhorted.

A young woman deacon, the Rev. Mrs. Patricia M. Park, read a prayer written for the new President by Bishop John A. Baden of Virginia. It asked that the President be given the "strength of spirit, body, and mind needed for the task; the wisdom to see, listen, and act for the good of all people."

She also recited the Prayer for the Despondent for the Nixons, a prayer that asks comfort for those who are "cast down and faint of heart amidst the sorrows and difficulties of the world."

At the conclusion of the service the Fords stayed to greet many of the 350 worshipers. Afterward, on the church steps outside, Ford thanked Dols for the sermon but noted that according to the printed program Mrs. Park had been scheduled to preach.

Dols later explained to reporters that he had been vacationing on Cape Cod and did not hear until Saturday afternoon that the new President would be in church on

Sunday. He flew back to the Washington area Saturday night and applied the final touches to his hastily prepared sermon. "Mrs. Park probably could have done a better job of preaching," he said. "But it was the President's first public appearance, and I thought I owed him the respect to come back and deliver the sermon."

Mrs. Park, an outspoken advocate for ordination of women to the priesthood—an issue causing controversy throughout the Episcopal denomination, told a *Christianity Today* reporter she was angry at first for being bumped in favor of her male superior on the staff. Some seminarians and teachers also expressed concern at what they considered was a putdown of womanhood by Dols, a liberal by reputation.

Ford would have heard Mrs. Park preach on the Beatitudes if Dols had not hurried back instead. Two weeks later Ford was again in the audience and this time Mrs. Park did preach, but on the women's issue in the denomination. She had just attended an emergency meeting of the House of Bishops in Chicago, where the rebel ordination of eleven women to the priesthood a month earlier in Philadelphia was invalidated. Some of the emotion generated by the issue came through loud and clear in her message. On his way out, Ford politely expressed appreciation to her for the sermon, but he voiced no opinion on the controversy.

Whether as President or Episcopalian, Ford would have plenty to think about in the months ahead.

That same week, on September 3, a story on Ford and Zeoli splashed onto the front page of the *Dallas Morning News*. Written by religion editor Helen Parmley and entitled, "A New Billy at the White House," the story quoted from a letter Ford had sent to Zeoli, congratulating him on the upcoming twenty-fifty anniversary of Gospel films. The President noted the influence of Christian films on church and family life, and then he stated:

> As you know, Billy, church has always meant much to me. The closeness of my family is also a great source of inspiration and challenge as we share our Christian faith.

...Because I've trusted Christ to be my Savior, my life is His. Often, as I walk into my office, I realize that man s wisdom and strength are not sufficient, so I try to practice the truth of Proverbs 3:5, 6.* And, Billy, I've experienced His leadership just as you have!

...I also want to thank you for taking the time to help me learn more about our Savior.

The widely quoted story clearly identified Ford as an evangelical on the issue of personal faith in Christ. "I've never been one to be ostentatious about my religious views," he told a reporter, "but I don't hesitate to say that Billy has had an impact on my perspective."

Hours before Ford's first nationally televised press conference, he and Zeoli met in the Oval Office for Bible study. They discussed several passages in Proverbs that deal with wisdom and good judgment.

Toward the end of Ford's vice presidency and in his first weeks as President, it was obvious that he was more outspokenly open about his faith than ever before. Was this the result of a sudden new experience, the kind of dramatic turning-around point in life that many evangelicals say happened to them in a time of spiritual crisis? No, replied Zeoli, the change was gradual, spanning years. "I have seen him grow in Christ and in Christian concern, yet his personality has not changed; he's as loving, open, and straight as when I first met him."

The *New York Times* noted approvingly Ford's attendance at a church as "a welcome change" from Nixon's practice of holding White House services. Turning the White House into a temporary house of worship made for a dangerous mixture of politics and religion, stated the editorial in a view not shared by many grass-roots church members and certainly not by the many evangelical leaders who attended those services. The *Times* felt Ford's "personal devoutness" and

---

*"Trust in the Lord completely; don't ever trust yourself. In everything you do, put God first, and he will direct you and crown your efforts with success" (*The Living Bible* version, the popular modern-language Bible Ford and Zeoli use in their private meetings).

public prayer references had a more sincere ring "because of his return to the old presidential custom of going to church, instead of having church come to him."

On Sunday, September 8, Ford again went to church, this time to an 8 A.M. communion service at St. John's Episcopal Church, across Lafayette Park from the White House. For security reasons Ford needed to vary his churchgoing habits. Also, in view of tighter schedules, St. John's was more conveniently located than Immanuel. (Every Pesident since James Madison's time has attended at least one service at St. John's, which was organized in 1815.)

After Communion, Ford returned to the Executive Mansion and less than three hours later announced his presidential pardon of Richard Nixon. The short speech contained six references to God, six to conscience, and allusions to angels, prayer, divine law, divine help, and the spirit. He implied that the former President's health, or even his life, was at stake, that Nixon would have great difficulty in obtaining a fair trial (a view at first contended but later concurred in by special Watergate prosecutor Leon Jaworski), and that the Nixons had suffered enough. Excerpts:

> Only the laws of God, which govern our consciences, are superior to [the Constitution]. As we are a nation under God, so I am sworn to uphold our laws with the help of God. And I have sought such guidance and searched my own conscience ... to determine the right thing for me to do....
>
> My conscience says it is my duty not merely to proclaim domestic tranquility, but to use every means I have to ensure it.
>
> I do believe ... that I cannot rely upon public opinion polls to tell me what is right.... I do believe with all my heart and mind and spirit that I, not as President, but as a humble servant of God, will receive justice without mercy if I fail to show mercy....

Like the rest of the nation, religious leaders were divided over the controversial action.

Evangelist Billy Graham said Ford acted with "decisiveness, courage, and compassion" in saving Nixon from prosecution, which "would have torn the country apart more than Watergate itself." Nixon, he added, "has already paid a terrible price."

Dr. W. Sterling Cary, president of the National Council of Churches, commended Ford for his desire to effect healing. But, insisted Cary, "this must be balanced by insisting on accountability for one's acts."

Eighty-four liberal clergymen (including three bishops) and well-known lay members of the Episcopal Church fired off a critical open letter, dissociating themselves from the religious aura which surrounded the issuance of the pardon and charging the act "actually extends the cover-up of which Mr. Nixon and others are charged." The pardon, they asserted, "was not in keeping with the church's teachings because it does not serve the truth."

Liberals were not the only ones critical of Ford's move. Conservative theologian Carl F. H. Henry cautioned that the pardon "confuses even more the distinction between justice and mercy at a time when both need to be clarified in American affairs." Pardon undisciplined by justice tends to be amoral, if not unethical, he stated.

While most of the Democrats in Congress lashed out at Ford, Georgia's Andrew Young—a black United Church of Christ clergyman active in the Washington prayer movement—spoke a word of moderation. The pardon amounted to a "certain mercy" to the country, he said, because it allowed Nixon to retire from public life "without being martyred." (Young was the only black congressman who voted for Ford's confirmation as Vice President. "I sense in him integrity that overrides all political considerations," he commented.)

Many questioned the timeliness of the pardon. Congressman John Anderson said that he didn't feel Nixon ought to go to jail if convicted but that the legal process should have been allowed to run its course. With no confession and no conviction, he argued, Nixon can propagate the false notion that he was hounded out of office.

According to Hugh Sidey, *Time's* man at the White House, Ford was cheered up a bit by a copy of a sermon he got in the mail. The sermon was by Duncan Littlefair, pastor of the Fountain Street Church in Grand Rapids, a clergyman long opposed to Ford's political philosophy. Littlefair said there was nothing dark or dishonorable about Ford's motives in pardoning Nixon. "Forgive when you can," he instructed. "Mercy and forgiveness cannot be weighed, measured, and balanced and counted—they must always be free, unearned, and undeserved."

Observed Sidey: "It was a shaft of light in the pardon gloom that spread over Ford's enlightened beginning."

There were immediate casualties as a result of Ford's action. One was his Gallup Poll popularity rating; it plummeted from 71 percent to 49 percent overnight.

"Instead of encouraging the healing process as he had hoped, Ford had reopened the Watergate wound and rubbed salt into the public nerve ends thus exposed," wrote former Detroit newsman Jerald F. terHorst in his biography on Ford. "With one short message, he erased the national euphoria that had attended his first thirty days in the White House."

Another casualty was terHorst himself, a Presbyterian elder, who was Ford's press secretary. He was opposed to the pardon, and he felt Ford had unfairly kept him in the dark about it, damaging his relationships with the White House press corps.

"Thus," he wrote Ford, "it is with a heavy heart that I hereby tender my resignation.... My prayers nonetheless remain with you."

Said terHorst to a *Time* reporter: "I couldn't in good conscience support the President's decision, even though I knew he took the action in good conscience."

In time the furor and debate over the pardon subsided, and the focus of public attention shifted at last to the far more serious problems gnawing at the nation: unemployment, inflation, the energy crunch, the international dollar drain, world hunger, the deteriorating situation in Southeast Asia, and the Middle East powder keg.

While most press coverage centered on Ford's handling of

these and other major affairs of state, there were occasional ethics-, conscience-, and religion-related sidelights affording further knowledge of the man.

Columnist Jack Anderson disclosed that an ethics seminar, complete with guidelines, was being designed for White House staffers. Commented Ford: "The code of ethics will be the example I set."

Ford's view that prayers should be permitted in public schools and that public aid should be extended to private schools (including parochial ones) earned him the displeasure of church-state separatists. His conditional clemency plan for draft resisters and military deserters, involving alternative-service obligations, was rapped by a number of churchmen who favored unconditional amnesty. These leaders included officers in the National Council of Churches and the majority of the Executive Council of the Episcopal Church. Liberals differed with him on his positions in favor of capital punishment and against abortion on demand.

When he nominated Nelson A. Rockefeller to be Vice President, Ford fell afoul of not only the conservatives in his Party but also of people upset over Rockefeller's divorce and remarriage in the early 1960s and of anti-abortion forces, from the Catholic bishops down.

Rockefeller, formerly governor of New York, is a member of the nondenominational Union Church in Pocantico Hills, New York. He also has close ties to Riverside Church in New York City, a congregation affiliated with both the American Baptist Convention and the United Church of Christ. He attributes his philosophic roots to the Christian teachings of both his parents. His father, John D. Rockefeller, Jr., taught a Sunday school class and led the family in prayers before breakfast every day.

Because of his family heritage, states Rockefeller in *Politics and Religion Can Mix!* (Broadman Press), he early "recognized politics not as an end, but a means to an end; that we must be guided by God's admonition that each of us is, indeed, his brother's keeper, and that we must put our belief to work through our public and political actions." The legacy from his parents for which he is most grateful, he says, "is the armor of Christian faith and love with which they equipped me...."

During his confirmation hearings, the wealthy Rockefeller revealed that between 1957 and 1974 he had contributed $24.7 million to charitable causes, including $782,763 to religious groups. More than $250,000 went to New York Catholic work. Ebenezer Baptist Church in Atlanta, pastored by Martin Luther King, Sr., received $132,312. The Pocantico Hills church got $29,596. A nonchurch item was $581,000 to the United Jewish Appeal.

Ford meanwhile continued his churchgoing, whether in Washington or on the ski slopes of Vail, Colorado, and he kept on giving a good word for God in his speeches.

Not everyone approved. Catholic priest William Clancy, a former editor of *Commonweal* and *Newsweek,* unleashed a bristling attack published by the *New York Times.* "We seem to expect our Presidents to worship publicly each Sunday, and our Presidents, in turn, find it easy and unembarrassing to suggest God's support for their policies," he chided. Ford, he went on, "shows signs of surpassing his predecessors in reliance on the Deity's advice," thus implying "that God is a member of his policy-planning staff." Both "the religious and the non-religious should demand an end to such nonsense," insisted Clancy. "Neither God nor man are honored or well served by it." He warned that God could be made "an accessory to the sordid" in such practice, and if so, "who shall grant a pardon to God?"

Historian Martin Marty sees the issue differently: "Shall [the voters] elect only representatives of the explicitly nonreligious minority? Are the godless automatically trustworthy? Shall the electorate force the pious to be hypocritical, to hide their religious faith when they are in the public realm? Some would ask their leaders to be compartmentalists, segregating their religion from their politics. But can people chop themselves up that way? Why should the best and noblest in religion be excluded from the public sphere?"

Ford shared his own thoughts on the topic at the 1975 meeting of the National Religious Broadcasters. Speaking about the First Amendment, he got enthusiastic applause when he implied that a national leader has as much a right to speak up publicly about his faith as anyone else. He said he subscribes to the separation of church and state clause but doesn't think it was intended "to separate public morality from public policy."

The next morning Ford gave a brief talk at the National Prayer Breakfast, telling how he was sustained by the power of prayer and appealing for prayers for the nation. Then he hurried back to the White House to meet with thirty-five leaders of the National Council of Churches. They represented all thirty-one member-denominations of the NCC, and they were there at Ford's invitation—the first time in more than a decade that NCC leaders were welcomed at the Executive Mansion. (The White House was off limits to main-line church leaders during the Johnson and Nixon years, mostly because of NCC-led criticism of the Viet Nam war.)

A passion for reconciliation and a willingness to compromise in order to achieve it is part of the Ford fabric. Communication is a necessary element in that arrangement, so Ford let the NCC leaders lay out their positions and grievances, and he even sparred with them at times. The churchmen told of their concerns in the areas of human rights, the world food crisis, and the economic and energy situations. They exchanged views on national priorities. Ford appointed an aide to act as his liaison with the NCC for matters that come up in the future, and he promised there would be other meetings, not only with them but also with Jewish, Catholic, and other Protestant leaders.

Both NCC general secretary Claire Randall and NCC president W. Sterling Cary commented favorably on the meeting, saying its greatest value lay in the channels of communication it opened.

Cary thanked the President for his openness and for his "willingness to enter into dialogue with those he didn't necessarily agree with." He closed the session with a prayer for guidance for the President, "who does not have the luxury of simplistic solutions," and for a "day of healing, not only for our land but for the world."

Much has been written in the press about Ford's positive qualities: his friendliness, his relaxed manner, his good-natured sense of humor, his love of life, his determination and discipline, his unwillingness to hold a grudge. There is an aspect of his life, however, that is hidden from public view. It is no less real than the other, and it may account for much of what we do see. The Bible teaches that the testing of one's faith produces patience and stability, a process wrought out in pain and perseverance. The vexing problems, the frustrations, the daily pressures of the office, and closer to home, his wife's bout with cancer—they can take a horrendous personal toll, or they can be the crucible out of which something more durable emerges.

But Gerald R. Ford does not face his trials alone. One day an aide entered the Oval Office without knocking and found the President kneeling by a chair—praying.

Back in his days as Vice President he talked about the tests of life during a House prayer breakfast where he'd been invited to speak. He implied that troubles make people reexamine their spiritual resources and relationships, thus opening the way to greater strength and blessing. Then he led his audience of fifty in prayer:

"Lord, we thank you for the stumbling blocks and obstacles you have set before us. We know that we must never stop asking ourselves the question, 'Where does Christ stand in my life? in the center or the fringe?' "

At the meeting of the National Religious Broadcasters referred to earlier, Ford suddenly became choked with emotion as he concluded his address with the familiar words from the third chapter of Proverbs: "Trust in the Lord with all thine heart ... and he shall direct thy paths."

That, said he, "is what I have tried to do, and will try to do, as President."

CHAPTER TWO

From Aldersgate to Watergate

Ironically, it was through Watergate that Washington's God movement first got national exposure. Reporters, tracking stories of Watergate figures who had experienced religious transformation, found the capital's prayer group movement and evangelical leaders behind it. Some of the resulting accounts and columns were critical, even sarcastic; most were fair. The matter of White House religion came under new scrutiny. Bible quotes were tossed around during the televised Senate Watergate hearings. Religious and political thinkers in and out of Washington pondered aloud what Watergate suggested about America's moral condition.

In a sense, Watergate itself was a religion story. Its roots lay in violations of the Ten Commandments, and its implications led to spiritual introspection on the part of many across the land.

Thou shalt have no other gods before me. A number of Watergate figures traced their fall to misplaced loyalties. For some, self-ambition crowded out considerations of conscience. Others said loyalty to the White House and the man in it superseded everything else: if an act was good for the Administration, it was good.

Thou shalt not covet ... anything that is thy neighbor's [including his private files], and, *Thou shalt not steal.* Somehow it never occurred to certain otherwise responsible persons that what was wrong legally was also wrong morally.

Thou shalt not bear false witness against thy neighbor. Perjury

37

figured in both the Watergate break-in and cover-up trials. People unwilling to accept responsibility for their own actions tried to shift the blame to others. Guilty parties denied their roles, in effect saying the witnesses were lying.

Thou shalt not take the name of the Lord thy God in vain. Whether this commandment is seen as an injunction against hypocrisy or merely a proscription against profanity, which may be an evidence of hypocrisy, the record abounds with examples of both.

Their lives reduced to rubble, several key Watergate personalities eventually faced up to such moral and spiritual issues, and they turned to God for answers.

JAMES W. McCORD, JR.

One such person is James W. McCord, Jr. One of the seven Watergate break-in defendants, McCord was going through hell as 1973 began. The trial was set to begin Monday, January 8. He had been unsuccessful in an attempt to make the government drop its case against him, and he in turn had rejected plea-bargaining attempts by the prosecution. Word had been passed to him from higher up: keep your mouth shut and plead guilty; your family will be cared for, and you'll get executive clemency within a year—along with money and a job.

This demand hadn't set well with him. The attempts of his superiors to cover their tracks at his and the others' expense irritated him. Moreover, no act of the President and no amount of money could undo the hurt Watergate had caused his wife Ruth and their three children. (One daughter was enrolled at the University of Maryland, another was attending classes for the mentally handicapped at a Catholic school, and their son was a cadet at the Air Force Academy.)

The balding, moon-faced McCord, in his mid-fifties, had angrily rejected an attorney's suggestion that he implicate falsely the Central Intelligence Agency in an attempt to halt the ongoing investigation. "If the Watergate operation is laid at the CIA's feet where it does not belong, every tree in the forest will fall," he warned in a letter to John J. Caulfield, a White House aide and officer of the Nixon campaign's Committee to Re-Elect the President (CRP).

For twenty years the Texas-born McCord had worked for the CIA, the last eight as a high-level CIA security chief, and before that he'd spent five years with the FBI. After retiring from the CIA in 1970, he organized a private security firm. In late 1971 he signed on as security director for the CRP.

The McCords attended First Baptist Church in downtown Washington for some years, then switched to a Methodist church near their home in the Maryland suburb of Rockville. A valued worker, McCord served on the church's administrative board and helped lead a ministry to the elderly. Pastor Walter Smith described him as "one of the best half-dozen people in our church."

Early on Saturday, June 17, 1972, three years after McCord began attending the Rockville United Methodist Church, he and his surveillance team were arrested. It happened during their second break-in at Democratic national headquarters in Washington's Watergate office-apartment-hotel complex.

Crushed and embarrassed, the McCords avoided acquaintances and dropped out of church. In their struggle to handle the ordeal, however, they discovered they needed God as never before. They accepted an invitation to go along with some friends to Fourth Presbyterian Church, a large suburban church where they could have substantial anonymity if they chose. They would be greeted with smiles, but no one would pry. Many government leaders attended, hence the congregation was not celebrity conscious, explained the friends.

On January 7, the day before the trial opened, the McCords again visited Fourth Church. White-haired pastor Richard Halverson, a respected long-time figure on the Washington evangelical scene, that day began a series of sermons on the lordship of Christ.

Halverson's first sermon in the series was based on the eighth chapter of Romans. Summarized, it went something like this:

We are living in a world under tension. God and His people are engaged in a struggle with the forces of evil. We all have within us a bent toward evil. It shows up in our wish to be our own god, setting up our own standards and plans apart from

Him, acting as we please. When leaders do this, the results are compounded, and as one rises in leadership the peril increases. Because of our defection from God, we are subject to frustration, futility, and trouble. How we handle it is the crucial question. The Christian knows that God will ultimately triumph in the world, and that in the meantime He will work out everything for good in the lives of those who love Him. True, we must recognize our failures, but we must also accept His forgiveness. Only as we place complete trust in Christ can we experience both security and freedom amid the tribulations of life.

The sermons over the next five Sundays expanded those themes, and Halverson—who did not know McCord was in the audience—pounded them home. "If we profess Christ as Lord," challenged the minister, "what evidence do we give that we are sincere in that profession, that we are not phony, that we are not hypocrites?" McCord was convinced that God was trying to tell him something. At some point during this period McCord the Hypocrite became McCord the Honest-Hearted.

Halverson's messages, said McCord later, "provided at a very critical time a spiritual undergirding for our family." Also, there were friends who had "a real capacity to understand." Ruth McCord credited her emotional survival in part to the loving concern and daily prayers of the nuns at her daughter's school.

The break-in trial lasted sixteen days. White House consultant E. Howard Hunt, a former CIA agent and one of the overseers of the Watergate ploy, and the four Cubans arrested with McCord all pleaded guilty. It was later learned that large sums of money had been channeled to them. Former White House aide G. Gordon Liddy, Hunt's partner in Watergate, and McCord both pleaded innocent. McCord through his attorney contended that he had acted under duress, "breaking a law to avoid a greater harm," namely, violence against the President and other officials. Judge John Sirica denounced this argument and refused to let the jury hear it.

Three times during the trial McCord and CRP official Caulfield met secretly on the Virginia side of the Potomac

River. Caulfield was worried: FBI agents were digging up links between the break-in and "a massive campaign of political spying and sabotage" involving high Administration officials, reporters were hot on the trail, and too many witnesses were being called to testify at the trial. Take clemency, urged Caulfield. "The President's ability to govern is at stake. Another Teapot Dome scandal is possible.... Everybody else is on track but you." McCord balked.

As the trial progressed, President Nixon was inaugurated for a second term and a week later announced the peace settlement in Viet Nam under which the American prisoners of war would soon come home. On January 30, 1973, after deliberating only ninety minutes, the jury found Liddy and McCord guilty on all counts. Sirica, convinced that the full story had not come out at the trial, deferred sentencing until March in hopes that more information would surface. A week after the trial concluded, the Senate set up a seven-member panel to look into Watergate and related matters. North Carolina Senator Sam Ervin, a Bible-quoting Southern Presbyterian in his seventies, was named chairman.

On March 18, five days before the sentences were to be handed down, McCord returned home from Fourth Church wrestling with a decision. Without telling his lawyer, he drafted a letter the next day and delivered it to Judge Sirica. In it he charged that he and the other defendants were under "political pressure" to plead guilty and remain silent, that perjury had been committed at the trial, and that higher-ups involved in the break-in had escaped unnamed.

McCord turned down a last-ditch money offer by Caulfield, and in successive appearances before Sirica, investigators, the grand jury, and the Ervin committee (he was its first public witness), he spelled out what he knew. He charged that CRP deputy director Jeb Magruder, presidential counsel John Dean III, and Attorney General John Mitchell had prior knowledge of the Watergate plot, and he implicated special presidential counsel Charles W. Colson, Jr.

The rest is history. Where there had been only leaks and an occasional spurt before, now a watergate was opened, and the dammed-up truth began to flow in force. In time it would become a flood that would sweep Richard Nixon right out of the White House.

Time felt McCord had written the letter to escape sentencing. Indeed, McCord—sentenced to two and one-half to eight years in prison—was able through appeals and delays to avoid incarceration for all but a few weeks of the next two years. He insists, however, that his motivation came from getting his spiritual-ethical house in order, thanks in large part to Halverson's sermons.

Watergate was a national and—for those involved—a personal tragedy. Yet, says McCord, some good has come from it. People are more concerned about cleaning up government, and officials in general are more sensitive to the moral requisites of public office. The system is not bad, he tells students; people are at fault when the system fails, "I was at fault." Through Watergate, he feels, perhaps God was dealing with our materialism and other evil ways in an attempt to move the nation closer to being what it should be.

CHARLES COLSON

Reporters who spotted Charles Colson in a White House corridor on a Thursday in mid-December, 1973, were incredulous when told he'd attended the bi-weekly White House prayer breakfast. Colson had resigned his post as special counsel to Nixon in March, when Watergate began to unravel, to devote full time to his law firm, located a block from the Executive Mansion (the Teamsters Union was among his clients). In the intervening months his name came up in the Watergate hearings but not conclusively, although it was rumored a grand jury was looking into a possible connection to the Fielding-Ellsberg break-in in Los Angeles.

Colson was remembered mainly as "once the toughest of the White House tough guys," as TV commentator Eric Severeid characterized him. For him to have religion was all but unbelievable. The story splashed onto front pages across America.

An only child, Colson was born in Boston of Episcopal parents, studied at Brown University, and worked for Republican Senator Leverett Saltonstall of Massachusetts while attending night classes at Georgetown Law School in

Washington. He formed his law firm in the early 1960s, worked in the 1968 Nixon campaign, and joined the White House staff as a political tactician in November 1969. Many, probably too many, of the "dirty tricks" in the 1970 and 1972 elections were attributed to him. He helped to formulate the White House "enemies list," and he may have been involved in the attempt to discredit John F. Kennedy's name through forged State Department documents.

Despite the "bad guy" reputation, Colson was a likeable, fun-loving practical joker who disregarded the caste system in White House circles. He was, however, an opportunist "without an ethical compass," observes former Colson aide Douglas Hallett, who knew him as a friend. Hallett claims Colson had opposed the Viet Nam War until he got the Administration job. Also, says Hallett, Colson was awed by the power around him, and he apparently drew no lines on what he would or would not do for Richard Nixon. It was Colson to whom Nixon addressed many of his memos instructing him to "get" certain political opponents.

Resolutely, Colson elbowed his way up from a one-secretary office to a staff of thirty. He even broke past the iron-clad protective hold that White House chief of staff H. R. Haldeman had on the Oval Office. In the last half of 1972, Colson saw Nixon more than any other staff member.

About the time he resigned in 1973, Colson on a trip to New England stopped by for a brief visit with Boston friend Tom Phillips, president of the Raytheon company, whom he hadn't seen in years.

"He was a totally different human being," Colson recalled later. He'd remembered Phillips as a hurrying, hard-driving, nervous corporate executive, forever pushing ahead. What lay behind the difference?

Phillips explained how during a time of great inner turmoil, mainly over self-identity and sense of fulfillment, he'd gone to the 1969 Billy Graham Crusade in New York City. After the meeting, while walking the streets late at night and trying to sort things out, suddenly everything clicked into place. The heavy reading he'd been into lately and what Graham had said now made sense. Indeed, *Christ* made sense.

That night, said Phillips, he committed himself to Christ, and his life changed vastly.

The ex-White House official responded with light skepticism. Faith might work for some, but a Christian couldn't survive in politics, he said. "When the other guy hits you, you've got to hit him back."

Yet Colson was impressed. Here was a man of intelligence and a background similar to his own, a man who came to this decision without being walked through it, a man at the top in a dog-eat-dog world who was at peace with himself and with God. Colson, who attended a Catholic church to please his wife Patty, hadn't given much thought to God. As tension built up over the next few months, though, he found himself wondering if Phillips might be on the right track after all.

In August, en route to a vacation spot in Maine, he again visited Phillips, and they picked up the conversation where they'd left it in March. "Chuck, don't you think you need Christ?" Phillips asked. "If so, let's talk about it." They read passages in *Mere Christianity,* a book by the late British thinker C. S. Lewis. One chapter jarred Colson, a chapter he would read and reread in the coming weeks. Entitled "The Great Sin," it was about pride and arrogance. Wrote Lewis:

> Pride gets no pleasure out of having something, only out of having more of it than the next man.... [God] wants you to know Him; wants to give you Himself. And He and you are two things of such a kind that if you really get into any kind of touch with Him you will, in fact, be humble—delightedly humble, feeling the infinite relief of having once got rid of all the silly nonsense about your own dignity which has made you restless and unhappy all your life. He is trying to make you humble in order to make this moment possible: trying to take off a lot of silly, ugly, fancy-dress in which we have all got ourselves up and are strutting about like the little idiots we are.[1]

Before Colson departed, he and Phillips prayed. On the

driveway outside, Colson said he felt the need to pray again. There by his car he asked Christ to come into his life.

"My first thought was, 'Will it last?' " he commented later. In Maine, he read books by Lewis and the Bible. He confirmed the driveway decision, submitting himself to Jesus, who had pursued self-denial to the point where He died in order that both His friends and enemies might have new spiritual life.

"Arrogance was the great sin of Watergate, the great sin of a lot of us, probably my greatest," he told audiences later.

Phillips asked Douglas Coe, a full-time worker in the Washington prayer group movement, to look in on Colson. Colson had seen the tall, dark-haired, freckle-faced Coe around the White House several times but had never known for certain what he did. Coe, in response to Phillips's request, visited Colson one day and chatted with him at length. That night Coe discussed the visit with members of his own prayer cell: Iowa Senator Harold Hughes, Minnesota congressman Albert Quie, former Texas congressman Graham Purcell, and their wives. It was decided that Hughes should take Colson under wing and help him along in the Christian life. Opposites philosophically and in background, Hughes the Dove and Colson the Hawk made an odd couple, but they became close friends. Thus it was that reporters saw Colson that day in December 1973, after the prayer breakfast in the White House. He was there at the invitation of Hughes, who was the featured speaker.

Colson's faith was tested in full view under TV klieg lights and as reporters pushed him with incessant, difficult questions. "If you're a Christian, why don't you confess your misdeeds?" "Don't you have an obligation to tell the truth about all you know, even about President Nixon?" "What do you intend to do to right the wrongs of the past?" (Unknown to the press, Colson indeed had been making amends to certain persons he'd wronged.)

Colson expressed dismay at the "lynch-mob atmosphere" and "lack of love" in Washington. At the same time, he confessed that until he met Christ, he'd had a get-that-guy attitude himself. But Christ changed that, he stated, and now there's love. Ex-aide Hallett, who was turned off by the "simplistic" aspects of Colson's new-found religious faith, nevertheless confirmed what his old boss was saying. Colson, he said, lost a lot of his "razor-sharp resentment and unharnessed aggression" after he professed Christ.

Colson was indicted in March 1974 for conspiracy to obstruct justice in the Watergate cover-up. He pleaded innocent, and his Christian friends enlisted nearly 100 persons, many of them members of Fourth Presbyterian Church, to help him put together 5,000 Xerox pages of press clips in an attempt to convince the court he couldn't get a fair trial anywhere in America. The charge was dismissed when he pleaded guilty to a similar charge in the Fielding-Ellsberg case. (One cheerful note during this period was Patty's decision to follow Christ after she joined a women's Bible study group.)

As noted by the nation's press, Colson's decision to plead guilty and the wording of his statement to the court expressing his willingness to talk were both thrashed out in a late-night meeting with his prayer partners Hughes, Purcell, and Coe (Quie, out of town, joined them by phone).

"There were tears shed," Hughes told reporters. "Here is a man who faces prison and disbarment." He said the group felt Colson might have gone free in a trial, "but he wanted to help in the cleansing process of the nation, to testify for the country and for Jesus Christ."

After Judge Gerhard Gesell handed him a $5,000 fine and a one- to three-year prison term, Colson told him: "I have committed my life to Jesus Christ. I can work for the Lord in prison or out of prison, and that's how I want to spend my life." True to his word, Colson organized a Bible study and prayer group among fellow inmates at the Alabama facility where he was sent.

When difficulties arose involving care of his widowed mother and a drug charge against one of his three children, Colson, in his early forties, was released January 31, 1975, after serving less than seven months. He expressed again his intention to become involved somehow in full-time Christian work, like his good friend Harold Hughes.

HAROLD E. HUGHES

The first elected member in the history of the Senate to give up his seat to engage in full-time Christian work was never implicated in the machinations of Watergate. Washington's "Mr. Clean" is considered here because of his role in providing spiritual support and counsel to Charles Colson. It was Hughes who sat with Colson when the ex-presidential aide was grilled by Mike Wallace on CBS-TV's "Sixty Minutes." When Wallace was pressing Colson to make moral judgments on Nixon and the White House tapes, it was Hughes who interrupted to point out that Colson was a "baby in Christ [without] full maturity or understanding. You are not wrong, Mike," Hughes added. "What you are saying primarily is, why doesn't a man arrive at his goal when he has just started the journey."

The Hughes-Colson relationship has been widely publicized. Many have marveled over how two men with such past political polarities can be so close. Hughes's answer is that Christian brotherhood transcends all human allegiances and differences.

But Hughes has also given spiritual counsel to scores of other Washington figures. In the final months of his Senate career, when the pall of Watergate hung blackest over Washington, he estimated spending a third of every day counseling people who wanted to talk about Christ. "They come to me, I don't go out to them," he asserted. "All kinds of people. Successes and failures. A Republican committeeman was just in here to pray. Multimillionaires and some who have little. We kneel right beside the couch in this office."

Those who come mean business, he insisted. "One man came in here the other day and confessed he was living with a woman who was not his wife. I said, 'Well, you'll have to do what God requires. You know what that means?' He said, 'Yes, I do.' He made a commitment to Christ and moved out."

Hughes was born in 1922 in Ida Grove, Iowa, and was raised a Methodist. He began drinking in high school, stopped attending church, dropped out of college after a year, got married at age nineteen, and went off to World War II. His drinking escalated after he got out of the service, but he was able to hold a job. He drove a semi-trailer truck, working his way up to become manager of the firm. On the side he got into various businesses of his own and eventually landed in state politics. All the time his alcoholism was getting worse.

In the early fifties, sick of the misery he was causing others, he vowed to stop drinking. He prayed, as he puts it, his "first honest prayer" in ten years: "God, help me; I cannot do it alone. If there is any purpose in my life, You've got to direct it; I can't." Something happened. "My heart was touched. I guess I had a John Wesley experience." John Wesley was the Anglican teacher and preacher who in 1738 had a dramatic spiritual-awakening experience while attending a service at the Aldersgate Chapel in London. Before that experience Wesley was a churchman with head knowledge of Christ but not an inward relationship to Him. He went on to found the Methodist Church.

Hughes never touched a drop after that day. His life style changed, and he disciplined himself in his new faith, frequently arising before dawn to pray and read the Bible. A big (6'3'' and 250 pounds), burly, gruff-voiced man who had growled at the world every day, he was transformed into "a tender, compassionate, understanding person whose special interests are the poor, the weak, the downtrodden, and those who have lost their spiritual way in life," as writer Lloyd Shearer put it.

He and his wife Eva Mae became active in church, and "using only the Bible," he taught a class of high school boys in a Methodist church in Des Moines after moving there. For a period of time he dabbled in parapsychology and attempts to communicate with the dead. He later blamed this on the failure of ministers to preach on the supernatural. They didn't seem to really believe in life after death or miracles, he said.

He was elected to three terms as Iowa's governor and at the late Bobby Kennedy's prodding, he ran for the United States Senate in 1968 and won. It is no secret that he had presidential aspirations.

Upon moving to Washington, Hughes became active in the city's prayer group movement and became one of its main boosters. He began attending meetings of a charismatic (neo-Pentecostal) congregation in Virginia ("they believe in the supernatural and in miracles at that place"). Here he received the "baptism of the Holy Spirit," accompanied by "the gift of tongues." (Hughes says he speaks in tongues only occasionally, and only in private praying.)

Hughes was known to the public at large for his outspoken, liberal views in Congress. These positions were drawn from the Bible, he maintains. His pacifism, for example, was grounded on his understanding of Christ and His command that one should love his enemies. Hughes believed that such commands should be applied nationally as well as personally.

Among his colleagues on Capitol Hill he was known for his decency and for "living the message he preaches," as Senator Thomas J. McIntyre of New Hampshire, a Catholic, characterized him. Another Catholic, New Mexico Senator Pete Domenici, thanked Hughes publicly "for what he has done for me, because he had made me ever more cognizant of my relationship to my God in terms of my role as senator."

Hughes snorts at skeptics who doubt genuine religious renewal is going on in Washington. "What are they looking for? People standing on the housetops and proclaiming the Lord? Let them look in rooms and basements and homes around here where men and women are meeting to pray, offering their lives to God, trying to reorder the priorities of their lives, making spiritual commitments."

There are those who wonder if Hughes really did the right thing in leaving the Senate; could he not have been more effective had he remained? Hughes replies that he is not out of the Senate altogether, and that he is able to help more people than before, thus increasing his usefulness.

"John Wesley said, Give me a hundred disciples and I will change the world," explained Hughes to writer Laurence Leamer. "If men come to Jesus Christ and love one another, the governments of the world will change.... If one man can change, one man can change the world."

Hughes has his eye—and heart—on those hundred people in the Senate and on hundreds of others around Washington, and he operates a rescue mission of sorts to reach them. Corruption and misery abound in the capital, he says, but God —and only God—can change all that, like He did for Colson.

JEB MAGRUDER

After McCord, Dean, and the turnabout Hunt began their fingerpointing, CRP director Jeb Magruder was the first to crack. He testified at the Watergate cover-up trial that he had lied to investigators during the break-in case, and he implicated a number of high officials in the cover-up. He pleaded guilty to perjury and conspiracy, for which he spent eight months in jail.

The handsome, boyish-faced Magruder joined the White House staff in 1969 after coordinating Nixon's southern California campaign. Attorney General John Mitchell named him to the CRP post in 1971. Magruder came from a middle-class Presbyterian home on Staten Island, New York. He maintained a B average at Williams College, where he took an ethics course under William Sloane Coffin, Jr., who later became known widely as the controversial chaplain of Yale. Coffin, a theological liberal, suggested that ethical actions might not always be in accord with biblical standards. Magruder got a C in the course.

In the Senate committee hearings Senator Howard Baker asked Magruder why, since he knew the proposed Watergate break-in was "illegal, inappropriate, and may not work," he went along with it. Magruder cited the ethics course under Coffin in his answer:

> During this whole time [when] we were in the White House and ... were directly employed with trying to succeed with the President's policies, we saw continuing violations of the law done by men like William Sloane Coffin. He tells me my ethics are bad. Yet he was indicted for criminal charges. He recommended on the Washington Monument grounds that students burn their draft cards and that we have mass demonstrations, shut down the city of Washington. Now here are ethical, legitimate people whom I respected. I respect Mr. Cof-

fin tremendously. He was a very close friend of
mine. I saw people I was very close to breaking the
law without any regard for any other person's pattern of behavior or belief. So consequently, when
these subjects came up, although I was aware they
were illegal, we had become somewhat inured to
using some activities that would help us in ac-
complishing what we thought was a cause, a legitimate cause.

Coffin, informed of the suggestion that his approach to
ethics helped Magruder rationalize his Watergate misdeeds,
fumed. "Jesus and Jimmy Hoffa both broke the law," he declared, "but there's a world of difference between what they
did. Whatever we did, we did in the open to oppose an illegal
war in Viet Nam. What he and the others did, they did behind
closed doors."

Chided *Christianity Today* editorially: "Apparently in his
presentation of situation ethics Coffin did not succeed in
communicating to Magruder his own ability to recognize that
while all situations are ethical, some situations are more ethical than others."

In an interview with journalist Studs Terkel for *Harper's,*
Magruder was more candid about his own responsibility:

A lot of people at the White House had a ... kind of
aggressiveness, ambition. They were more interested in power than money, more interested in
getting things done. Not just talking about them. I
became one of these people.... I subverted my personal feelings to what I felt was the President's desire. I think that's the root cause of Watergate....
It's a question of slippage. I sort of slipped right into
it. Each act you take leads you to the next act, and
you eventually end up with a Watergate....It starts
as a matter of public relations. You justify it in the
name of national security. And what comes out is
blatant lying. It starts as simple misrepresentation,
by the way in which you package your product.[2]

Magruder also made an interesting comment about the White House worship services which were taking place in those days: "It was very pleasant. Maybe it wasn't a great religious experience, but I always enjoyed going.... It was a form of stroking. We used it to fulfill our social obligations for a lot of people."

Religious faith apparently was not a strong factor in Magruder's decision to tell the truth at the cover-up trial. He admitted readily that it was mostly a matter of making "the best possible deal" for himself.

About this same time, however, he and his wife Gail began participating in a Bible study and prayer group at National Presbyterian Church, where they found deep supportive friendships. National's recently-arrived pastor Louis Evans and his wife Colleen took special interest in the Magruders, and the troubled couple committed themselves to Christ. The Evanses were close by when Magruder was sentenced, when he left for prison, and when he was released.

At this appearance before Judge Sirica for sentencing, Magruder made a statement:

> It has been nearly impossible for me to face the disappointment I see in the eyes of my friends, the confusion I see in the eyes of my children, the heartbreak I see in the eyes of my wife and, probably more difficult, the contempt I see in the eyes of others.... My ambition obscured my judgment.... Somewhere between my ambitions and my ideals I lost my ethical compass.

As he headed off for prison, the penitent Magruder told reporters he intended to spend part of his time studying theology. He had discovered that ethics, to be reliably operative, must be rooted in the absolutes of the Bible.

EGIL KROGH

The Watergate investigation uncovered the "Plumbers" unit, a secret White House task force set up in 1971 to investigate security leaks to the news media. In September 1971, four of the men later convicted in the Watergate break-in took part in a Plumbers operation. They broke into the office of Los Angeles psychiatrist Lewis Fielding to examine the files of Daniel Ellsberg, the former Henry Kissinger employee who leaked the Pentagon Papers.

The co-directors of the Plumbers were David Young, a Wheaton (Illinois) College graduate who had joined Kissinger's National Security staff in 1970, and Egil "Bud" Krogh, a member of the Christian Science church (as were H. R. Haldeman and John Ehrlichman). Young allegedly arranged access to secret State Department cables for E. Howard Hunt in the attempted Kennedy smear.

Young, refusing to talk about connections between the Fielding and Watergate break-ins, took the Fifth Amendment more than forty times before a House subcommittee. He also remained silent before a Los Angeles grand jury. He pleaded innocent in the 1973 Fielding-Ellsberg case in California, and that state's charges against him and Krogh were finally dropped in 1974. Young, who had meanwhile resigned from the White House staff, then left Washington to take up graduate study at Oxford.

The Chicago-born Krogh, a handsome outdoors type and mature looking for his mid-thirties, graduated from Principia College, a Christian Science school in Illinois, and from the University of Washington law school. He went to work for John Ehrlichman's law firm in Seattle, then followed Ehrlichman to the White House in 1969 to be the Administration's liaison man with the District of Columbia government. His specialties were transportation and crime prevention. District officials spoke highly of him, using such descriptives as "strong, honorable, effective."

The long hours and swirl of life in the capital took their toll. His two young sons would sometimes nap in the afternoon to wait up for him at night, but he would arrive home too exhausted and too uninterested to play husband and father. He and his wife Suzanne separated in 1970.

"The syndrome is so typical of the hard-charging young men in government and business," commented one of Krogh's government friends to a reporter. "You become blinded by the power, you begin to think that you're indispensable. Suddenly, family obligations seem unworthy of your talents."

In 1971 Krogh was named to direct the Special Investigations Unit (the Plumbers). One of their projects was to discredit Ellsberg. The break-in at the psychiatrist's office, which he had authorized, subsequently raised doubts and questions of ethics and justice that wouldn't go away. The search for answers led him back to his Christian Science faith from which he had drifted years earlier. Contemplation of religious belief brought some changes to his life. When he refused to authorize a wiretap in 1972, he was removed as head of the Plumbers. He was reconciled to his wife and began attending the White House prayer breakfast for lower-echelon executives. That summer he was nominated by Nixon to a post as an undersecretary of the Department of Transportation. Then came Watergate. It was only a matter of time, he knew, before the trial would lead to the Fielding break-in.

Krogh felt he should tell what he knew, but Ehrlichman instructed him to keep quiet on grounds of national security. When he received a summons to appear before the Watergate grand jury, John Dean allegedly told him, "You must lie like you've never lied in your life before." As a result, said Krogh later, he did not tell the jury the truth.

In April 1973, the Justice Department disclosed that Watergate figures had taken part in the Fielding break-in. The judge presiding at the Daniel Ellsberg-Anthony Russo trial in California, where they were charged with espionage, theft, and conspiracy, asked for anyone with information to come forward. Krogh at last obtained Nixon's permission to send the judge a statement detailing his role in the break-in. The statement resulted in the charges against Ellsberg and Russo being thrown out of court.

On May 9, 1973, Krogh resigned his government position and awaited the federal case against him. He intended to plead guilty and tell all, but his lawyer persuaded him to remain silent. He took the Fifth Amendment fifty-two times before a House panel. In November he was summoned before Judge Gerhard Gesell to explain the discrepancies between his declaration to the Watergate grand jury and his statement to the California judge. Krogh's lawyer moved for dismissal of the false-declaration charge that had been lodged against Krogh. He reasoned that since Krogh was under a White House order of secrecy he had no other choice but to lie.

Gesell exploded. "Lie?" he thundered. "Before an officer of the court?" He rejected the motion in a stern lecture and scheduled a trial two weeks hence.

Krogh, deeply affected by Gesell's remarks, took his family on a Thanksgiving holiday trip to historic Williamsburg, Virginia. He took a Phillips version New Testament along and spent a lot of time reading it and praying over what it showed him about himself. Until that time, he pointed out later, "the Bible had never really meant anything to me." He said it revealed to him a higher morality and showed him it was wrong to lie, even if the President asked him to. It also taught him to have sacred respect for others. The relics of Williamsburg reinforced this impression, reminding him how the nation's government had been designed to protect the rights of every individual.

"How can I continue to defend conduct that had stripped another person of his constitutional rights?" he wondered. In the New Testament Krogh also discovered the power of God that could enable him to translate ideals into reality.

On November 30, 1973, he went before Judge Gesell and pleaded guilty to the charge of conspiring to violate Dr. Fielding's civil rights. "I now feel that I cannot in conscience assert national security as a defense," he stated. He also indicated his willingness to testify in the Fielding and Watergate matters, but only after he was sentenced. He didn't want any leniency in exchange for information. Gesell gave him a six-month sentence.

Before leaving for the prison farm at Allenwood, Pennsylvania, Krogh met with Harold Hughes for prayer.

"I'm convinced that man knows Christ," Hughes reflected afterward.

SENATOR SAM J. ERVIN, JR.

One of the most colorful figures in the Watergate cast was Democratic Senator Sam J. Ervin, Jr., chairman of the Senate

Watergate committee and an elder in the First Presbyterian Church of Morganton, North Carolina. His country-style philosophizing and his frequent King James Bible quoting during the hearings won him both praise and censure. Piosity, charged many critics. Not so, defended Pastor John M. McCoy of the Morganton church, it was the real Ervin. "He has a firm grasp on Scripture and has committed to memory great sections of the Bible."

Hit several times with biblical admonitions by Ervin, John Ehrlichman rejoined that he read the Bible too but didn't go around quoting it. Senator Howard Baker, Ervin's Republican colleague on the committee and a Bible-reading elder in a Presbyterian church, gently implied that it was not in good taste to quote the Bible in public so much in support of one's personal views.

At one point, with CRP official Frederick LaRue in the witness seat, Ervin apparently saw embodied in him all the evasive, arrogant wrongdoers of Watergate. "Be not deceived," he admonished, quoting Galatians 6:7, "God is not mocked; for whatsoever a man soweth, that shall he also reap." The caucus room erupted in cheers and applause.

"It is ironic," commented United Methodist reporter Martha Man, "that in an era of evangelical influence in the White House, the evangelical's major weapon—the Bible— is the heavy artillery booming from the camp of the protagonist."

JULIE NIXON EISENHOWER

Christmas, 1973, was not a bright one for Julie Nixon Eisenhower. With the clamor over the White House tapes, the calls for impeachment, and all the unkind press coverage, a dark mood of despair was settling in on the First Family. It tore Julie up to see her dad getting beaten down and shredded more almost every day. Her mother managed to hide her loneliness and grief behind a stiff upper lip and an occasional forced smile, but Julie could sense the deep hurt.

Needing help to cope with all the pressures, Julie decided to seek help from Billy Graham when he came to preach at the White House Yule service two Sundays before Christmas. During the refreshment period following the service, Irene

Conlan, wife of a freshman Arizona congressman, introduced herself to Julie and invited her to attend a congressional wives' Bible study group that met at the Conlan home on Thursdays. When Julie mentioned the encounter to Graham during their counseling session, he encouraged her to attend.

The study group was led by Elinor Page, widow of a military officer and a lay worker with Campus Crusade for Christ. The studies dealt with matters of identity, with God's love and His plan for one's life, with who Christ is and how He can help with life's problems. These were subjects Julie wanted to know more about, so she showed up weekly at the Conlan home with Bible and notebook in hand.

One day in March 1974, as she was preparing for the next lesson, she suddenly realized that the Christian life cannot be lived apart from personal trust in Christ. Then and there, recalled Julie later, "I made a decision to invite Christ into my life."

She began attending services regularly at several evangelical churches in the suburbs. She found her greatest inspiration and support, however, in the group at the Conlan home and in a smaller group composed of Mrs. Conlan and three other women. The latter group met weekly in Julie's office in Washington to pray and study the Bible.

Julie gave her first public testimony of faith at a women's meeting during a National Religious Broadcasters' convention in Washington in January 1975. Becoming a follower of Christ did not end her problems, she acknowledged, but it did provide a basis for dealing with them. Love, she found, displaced the bitterness she once had toward others. "My whole life has really changed." She said she still encounters periods of discouragement when it "is difficult to trust [God] as I should." Yet, she affirmed, the simple knowledge "that God loves and accepts me completely" helps her get over the rough spots.

A few days later she repeated her testimony to a Campus Crusade-sponsored gathering of some 2,500 society leaders in Florida. Nancy Ziegler, wife of Nixon press secretary Ron Ziegler, also described how she had become a Christian through the Bible studies at Mrs. Conlan's home. When the invitation to "receive Christ" was extended, scores from the audience reportedly responded.

So the chain response resulting from the spiritual commitments of people caught up in the wide swirl of the Watergate
tragedy continues. The most asked question remains: What
of former President Nixon, the Quaker son of an evangelical
Sunday school teacher? It is known that he made a Christian
commitment in his youth and was active in his home church
in southern California before becoming involved in a controversy over social dancing at Whittier College, a Quaker
school. Nixon's friendship with Billy Graham is better known,
as are the celebrated and oft-controversial White House religious services held while he was in the White House.

As the Watergate noose was tightening around Nixon's
neck, two high Washington figures in the prayer network
tried to arrange a no-holds-barred prayer meeting with the
beleagured president. A date was reportedly set, but a sudden
change in the president's schedule caused cancellation.

The former president's faith remains a private matter with
the enigmatic man who will be judged by history and by God.
Perhaps Billy Graham—who maintained all along that he was
a friend of Nixon's but never close—knows more than any
other person outside of the family. Graham, who visited the
lonely former president at his San Clemente residence in
early 1975, will say only that Nixon is becoming "more deeply
religious."

The verdict of history is yet to be pronounced on Watergate. We can only say now that some good has resulted from
the tragedy for which the nation has paid such a terrible
price. That good must include those who have had their lives
redirected by new-found faith.

More good can result to us all if we remember the
lessons—and heed Sam Ervin's warning given after his retirement from the Senate. "America," he declared, "will im-
peril her existence as a free society if she ever forgets the
tragic truth Watergate teaches in respect to the need for integrity in the political process."

Everyone recognizes that need for integrity. How can it be
achieved and ensured? With God's help, say those who found
out for themselves.

CHAPTER THREE

Standing in the Need of Prayer

Except for state funerals and quadrennial inaugurations, Washington's political establishment comes together only twice a year: for the presidential State of the Union address to Congress and for the National Prayer Breakfast. Launched in 1953 by International Christian Leadership with the blessings of President Dwight Eisenhower, the Breakfast is the capital's religio-political event of the year. It is held in early February, usually just before Groundhog Day; an appropriate time, a wag muses, because like the proverbial groundhog some politicians come out for God only once a year.

If the next Breakfast follows tradition, the President, Vice-President, Chief Justice, House and Senate Majority Leaders, heads of the House and Senate prayer groups, Billy Graham, and special guests will be at the head table in the Washington Hilton's largest banquet room. Before them will be more than 2,500 lesser powers: senators, representatives, cabinet makers, judges, top-echelon bureaucrats, foreign dignitaries, and a high level assortment of political, business, labor, and religious leaders from across the country. Even the Soviet ambassador has attended.

The affair is so prestigious and the audience so influential that thousands of Americans covet the engraved invitations. Even a snake handling preacher from Tennessee requested an invitation so that he might demonstrate his gift and revive the nation.

The program always carries an ecumenical and political balance. For example, at the 1975 Breakfast—when the dignitaries spooned only oatmeal "as a symbolic recognition of pressing human needs that exist in many parts of the world"—John Dellenback, a Presbyterian and a former Republican Congressman from Oregon, presided as chairman. Mayor Walter Washington of Washington, a Baptist and a Democrat, offered the opening prayer. Evangelist Billy Graham, who has come to be a Breakfast fixture, gave a brief "Call to Fellowship," in which he pegged this period in the nation's history as the "fourth great crisis" (the other three being the Revolutionary War, the Constitutional Convention, and the Civil War). Rep. Richardson Preyer (D.-N.C.), a Presbyterian, and Senator Sam Nunn (D.-Ga.), a Methodist, brought greetings from the House and Senate breakfast groups respectively. Judge Oliver Gasch of the U.S. District Court (chairman of the Washington City Prayer Breakfast Group) read Psalm 1, and Elizabeth Hanford, a commissioner of the Federal Trade Commission, read from Hebrews. A prayer for national leaders was given by Florida's Presbyterian Governor Reuben Askew.

President Gerald Ford spoke briefly, as has been the custom of past chief executives, and recalled that prayer "to me, as to many of my predecessors, is a terribly important source of confidence and strength." Rep. Albert H. Quie, a Lutheran, was the principal speaker, declaring that the answer to political animosities is "Christ in us" producing "love for each other." Alluding to differences existing between President Ford and the Congress on solutions for the economic crisis and other matters, Quie said that "if we can love each other, then I think we can blend our ideas together for the betterment of the people...." Former Senator Harold Hughes, a Democratic and a charismatic Methodist, gave the closing prayer.

Such representation has fueled charges that the Breakfast transgresses the principle of separation of church and state. It does not, contend its backers. The sponsoring Senate and House prayer groups are unofficial voluntary groups, and those who attend the breakfasts do so as private citizens, they point out. (Behind-the-scenes legwork and promotion is handled by workers associated with Fellowship House.)

Another criticism is that the Breakfast is merely "piety on the Potomac," an expression of bland civil religion devoid of a cutting prophetic edge. Critics voicing this objection tend to view it as little more than just another social gathering that has no significant impact on national life.

Some feel Billy Graham allowed himself to be used—especially by former President Richard Nixon. But it would have been difficult for the evangelist to stand apart from Nixon at the 1974 Breakfast had he wanted to. On the preceding afternoon Graham was in his room at the Hilton when a call came from Nixon asking him to come to the White House so they could travel together to the breakfast. "What do you do when the President asks you to come?" defended Graham to an interviewer later. A White House driver had picked him up early in the morning, and after a brief visit, Nixon and the evangelist rode the presidential limousine to the Hilton, where reporters and news photographers were waiting.

Nixon spoke briefly at the observance—as presidents usually do—remarking, "Too often we are a little arrogant... What this nation needs to do is to pray in silence and listen to God to find out what He wants us to do."

Harold Hughes gave the main address, perhaps the most stirring sermon heard by Washington politicians in recent years. Recalling his spiritual deliverance from alcoholism, the ex-truck driver exclaimed: "I was beaten to my knees in despair. I cried out to God, and from that moment my life changed." Thundering like an Old Testament prophet, he declared that America "has wallowed in luxury and dirtied its nest." He called for repentance, assuring that God could use men's "indiscretions" to "build up His people."

"The Word of God came in Jesus Christ and revealed eternal life," Hughes assured. "The debt has been paid in the blood of our Savior."

At the end he asked everyone to join hands around tables and pray audibly for renewal and whatever came to mind as a need. The distinguished individuals glanced uneasily at one another, then one by one people began extending hands to each other. Only those at the head table refrained.

For a moment there was silence, then a voice here and another there began to pray, then others, and soon there was a crescendo of voices simultaneously thanking God and imploring Him for help in personal and national life. Finally, Hughes spoke a closing prayer into the microphone, and the crowd quieted. When he sat down no one stirred, no clinking of cups marred the hush. Then in the stillness someone began applauding and as one the great body rose and accorded Hughes a long ovation.

No one could remember a Breakfast when there had been such participation in prayer. Several observers commented that if Hughes had given a Billy Graham-style invitation to receive Christ, hundreds would have responded. Later, in retrospect, Hughes would see the changeover in the White House and the resulting new climate of trust and cooperation as direct answers to such prayers.

During the same week as the prayer breakfast a number of "leadership seminars" are held in which Christian politicians discuss spiritual issues and involvement of Christians in government. For several years Campus Crusade for Christ has arranged for selected college student leaders to come to Washington for these seminars. Some are now working in Washington as a result of these seminars.

One is Scott McBride, who came in 1965 when he was president of the student body at Stanford University. "I thought the prayer breakfast was hypocrisy," he recalls, "but I wanted to meet important people. I roomed with Charlie Powell, the student body president at the University of California in Berkeley, who had become a Christian the year before. Charlie took me to some of the small groups where I discovered my need for Christ. Later I did accept Christ and felt God leading me back to Washington."

Numerous smaller prayer breakfasts have spun off the big Washington fete. While boosters do not keep records, it is estimated that about forty governors and some 1,000 mayors host annual prayer breakfasts across the U.S. Abroad, several governments have held their own national prayer breakfasts, modeled after Washington's. South Korea has had eight in a row (the 1974 observance was boycotted by some religious leaders in protest against President Park Chung Hee's alleged repressive policies). Bolivia held its first in 1974 with Argentine-born Evangelist Luis Palau as guest speaker. The Bolivian breakfast had its origins in missionary David Farah's prison visits to deposed President Hugo Banzer. When Banzer was restored in a counter coup he approved Farah's suggestion for a prayer breakfast, and most of the key members of his government participated.

The National Prayer Breakfast and the defunct White House services have been highly publicized. But there are more than seventy lesser known prayer and Bible study groups composed of government people meeting regularly throughout the year, plus numerous other small cell groups of three to six persons or so who meet weekly for spiritual enrichment. More than twenty groups schedule meetings in rooms of the Capitol and adjacent congressional office buildings, seventeen in the mammoth Pentagon, and some three dozen scattered throughout the cavernous agencies, from the State Department to the Environmental Protection Agency. They meet weekly or bi-weekly with attendance ranging from approximately twenty to eighty, sometimes more on special occasions. Participants include President Ford, White House aides, cabinet members, senators and congressmen, judges—including at least one Supreme Court Justice (William H. Rehnquist), congressional staff, admirals, generals, officers of lesser rank, CIA and other intelligence operatives, and various career specialists ranging from lawyers to secretaries and even janitors and waitresses.

Membership of some groups is according to rank or leadership level. For example, before attending to strategic military affairs of global influence, about a dozen admirals, generals, and top defense department officials meet each Tuesday at 6:30 A.M. in the Secretary of the Army's private Pentagon dining room for coffee, doughnuts, and ninety minutes of prayer and Bible study.

Other groups are not so stratified, such as one in the

Department of Transportation (DOT) that includes Coast Guard personnel from an admiral down to enlisted men as well as DOT engineers, office secretaries, and other transportation-related workers.

Most groups meet in offices, around conference tables, or in dining rooms on government property, although none is officially sponsored by any governmental agency. Some are mobile, moving on short notice when the regular room is preempted for official business. Most advertise by word of mouth, except in the Pentagon where printed schedules of all groups are distributed at intervals. A few meet in downtown restaurants and in churches.

Four groups are known to convene regularly in the White House. One is the Ford-Laird-Quie-Rhodes cell. Another is for women below the executive level and meets Wednesday mornings at 7:30 in the Family Theater where the presidential family views movies. A second group for women, mainly secretaries, meets in the nearby new Executive Office Building. The fourth group is for cabinet and sub-cabinet officers, presidential aides, other high level executive appointees, and a few former White House personnel who enjoy being back with their friends. (This is the meeting where Charles Colson was headed when he was spotted by reporters who wondered what the former Watergate figure might be doing back in the White House.)

The catalyst for the high-level White House group was the late David Lawrence, editor of *U.S. News and World Report*. John Nidecker, a presidential aide at the time, remembers: "Lawrence met with five of us in the summer of 1971. He was Jewish but believed in Christian principles and had been active in a Capitol Hill group. He talked about how President Eisenhower had relied on prayer for assistance in difficult times. He gave some reasons why we should have our own group here. So, starting with six, we began meeting for breakfast each Thursday morning at eight. Thursday was the day Lawrence could be with us. And Federal Reserve Chairman Arthur Burns could come that day. He is Jewish, too, but can speak more knowledgeably on Christ than many Christians."

The group grew to about thirty, with up to sixty sometimes coming. It was soon decided to meet only twice monthly because of conflicting meetings. With this growth informal discussion gave way to having a speaker who fields a few questions afterwards.

Nidecker, an Episcopalian, has been the coordinator since the beginning. Responsibility for securing speakers and sending out invitations rotates monthly among cabinet members. Speakers usually come from within the group, but outsiders like Senators Hughes and Hatfield—both favorites—have spoken. Billy Graham is the only clergyman who has addressed the group. Leaders think religious professionals "tend to make a Sunday service out of a mid-week meeting." Washington prayer-movement leader Doug Coe usually attends, occasionally bringing along others who give testimonies of their faith.

Participants reflect a broad religious diversity ranging from Protestant evangelicals to members of the Mormon and Jewish faiths. Foreign guests including a Buddhist official and the secretary of the Israeli Parliament have attended. Some of the most noted regulars have been: former Attorney General William Saxbe (now Ambassador to India), Agriculture Secretary Earl Butz, Commerce's Harry Dent, HEW's Caspar Weinberger, and economist Arthur Burns. Nixon's speech-writing "house Jesuit," John Mclaughlin, also attended. The colorful George Romney, a Mormon, attended regularly when he was in the cabinet, and was a favorite speaker.

The program begins at eight A.M. sharp, with the leader for the month calling on someone to lead in a prayer of thanks. Breakfast is served and then at 8:20 the speaker is introduced. Topics vary according to the speaker's background and spiritual experience. The talk may be a simple evangelical message, an ecumenical extolling of the brotherhood of men and the fatherhood of God, a ringing patriotic narrative of how the Founding Fathers established "one nation under God," or a discourse on a political or sociological issue related to religion.

For example, Secretary Dent, a Mormon, one day

presented his thesis on church and state: the Founding Fathers never intended that God and Christian faith be left out of American government; they just did not want a church-state marriage such as existed in England. He went on to give a history of the biblical origin of Christianity and how it spread in time to the Western world. After a short question-and-answer discussion, everyone stood and joined hands as Dent led in prayer for the administration, the judiciary, and for individual needs in the group.

Richard Nixon never attended. "He told us he prayed in private," one of his former aides says. "We never pressed him, for we felt the group would be inhibited if he did come."

Just after Gerald Ford took office Nidecker informed him about the prayer group and invited him to come. "I'll be there," he promised, "but because of my schedule, I'll have to leave before the speaker begins." That Tuesday morning Harold Hughes was again the speaker. Ford stayed for the entire session.

Tape recording the sessions is not permitted and discussion of partisan politics is banned from the sessions. "If someone should start a political speech," coordinator Nidecker declares, "I would immediately call for the closing prayer."

The Senate and House prayer groups, which have been meeting over thirty years, assemble on Wednesday and Thursday mornings respectively in the Capitol dining rooms instead of the congressional prayer room. That small room, just off the rotunda that connects the House and Senate wings of the Capitol, was built under the leadership of folksy Sam Rayburn during his term as Speaker of the House. It is occasionally used for private prayer, but its most popular use is probably as a wedding chapel.

The congressional prayer groups are always restricted to members and their official chaplains. "That's so they can be themselves without having to explain to a reporter," a congressional aide says. Still, only a small minority—about 10 percent of the 435 House members and perhaps 20 percent of the 100 senators—attend the weekly prayer sessions.

The format is similar for both groups. "Our House group starts with the chaplain leading in prayer," Rep. Jim Wright

(D.-Texas) explains. "After we eat, a member brings a short devotional followed by informal commentary from around the tables."

Because Senators tend to be older than Representatives, the Senate group is said to resemble a senior men's Sunday school class in a small town. Old timers like Randolph of Virginia, Stennis of Mississippi, and Curtis of Nebraska are comfortable with each other. Political differences (men with such opposing views as Strom Thurmond and Mark Hatfield attend) are left outside so that cameraderie and good fellowship may prevail inside the private dining room. Although they pray for the country and for wisdom in voting on legislation, most of their entreaties are for the personal needs of one another.

"We have a happy comradeship around the table during the meal," says Jennings Randolph, the only Seventh Day Baptist in Congress. "When we stand and hold hands, I feel a strength flowing among us. Wednesday is always the best day of the week for me."

Rep. John Duncan (R.-Tenn.) agrees. "We may be partisan adversaries in floor debate, but in our prayer groups we develop respect for one another as we discover what we really are down deep."

But at least one Senator, unnamed in a story by the *New York Times's* Edward Fiske, feels there is too much emphasis on personal piety and not enough consideration of what Christians in government should do about serious social problems. This senator thinks there "are too many talks on the special guidance America has had because those pious men in Philadelphia waited for the Holy Spirit to lead them."[1] (The "pious" framers of the Declaration of Independence affirmed "a firm reliance on the protection of divine Providence" for the "support" of the Declaration.)

In addition to the two general prayer groups for the Senate and House there are smaller prayer cells in which a number of legislators are involved.

One of these cells includes Reps. Guy Vander Jagt (R.-Mich.), James Symington, Jr. (D.-Mo.), John Dellenback, and Andrew Young, the black Democrat from Georgia.

"We discussed issues from a Christian perspective," Dellenback, a Presbyterian elder, notes. "For instance, one day we asked ourselves: What does our faith say to the school prayer amendment? Two said they intended to support it. I felt it was a mistake. We were all earnest in our faith, all trying to find what God wanted, even though we seemed to be getting different signals." (The proposed amendment was subsequently defeated, with many prayer supporters voting for its defeat. Their reasons included: possible violation of the establishment-of-religion clause in the Constitution, infringement of first amendment rights and imposition of hypocrisy by forcing nonbelievers to pray.)

Two other prayer cells, the congressional cell Gerald Ford met with two days before becoming president and the one that influenced Charles Colson's guilty plea, have received wide publicity. The supportive role these groups play in times of crisis is not as well known, but was dramatically demonstrated on the day Colson was sentenced. The members of his prayer cell stood with him both in the courtroom as he faced the judge and outside when he told reporters, "I have committed my life to Jesus Christ. I can work for the Lord in prison or out of prison, and that's how I want to spend my life."

Besides providing strength gained from supporting one another, the prayer groups help politicians "understand one another," according to Rep. Albert Quie. "You have to be honest in a small group," he says. "You can't con your brother. You go deeper in the Christian life."

CHAPTER FOUR

Guidance in the Bureaucratic Maze

At 6:50 on a balmy Thursday morning blond, blue-eyed Carl Miller kisses his wife and four children good-bye in suburban Rockville, Maryland, and joins a car pool for the short ride to a bus stop parking lot. There he boards a chartered Metro bus which carries fifty government workers into the bureaucratic beehive of southwest Washington.

By 8:30 Miller, holder of a master's degree in nuclear engineering from the Massachusetts Institute of Technology, is in the radiation lab at the sprawling Environmental Protection Agency (EPA). He will spend much of his day evaluating raw field data sent in by EPA field workers who have been monitoring the radiation levels of newly installed nuclear reactors.

At 12 o'clock he picks up his bag lunch, takes the elevator to the ground level shopping center where he purchases a dessert, then walks across a parking lot to the modern new Westminster Presbyterian Church. With less than 140 members it barely survives in the midst of high-rise apartments and agencies that employ 75,000 people. Most of these workers, like Miller, live miles away and attend suburban churches.

Using the key entrusted to him by the pastor, Miller opens the door for a few fellow-EPA people who have congregated; several others are just arriving. They walk downstairs to the church fellowship room where they spend their lunch hour eating, discussing a Bible passage, sharing mutual job and family concerns, and praying for one another's needs. As is often the case, Miller meets a fellow believer from his own department of 600 people whom he hadn't known before. And, not surprisingly, he hears of a new EPA believer; a secretary who was introduced to Christ by her car pool partner.

Fifteen minutes by taxi across the Capitol Mall and just beyond the towering Washington Monument another group is meeting on the third floor of the huge State Department building. As at EPA this group of about sixty is an assorted mix of employees. A man in a janitor's apron sits beside a manager. A file clerk chats with a specialist from the Agency for International Development (AID) who has just returned from Asia.

Lorren E. Hackett, a thirtyish black with a glistening Afro, introduces the leader for the day, a white. Charles Coleman, a government consultant who was once a verification expert on the SALT disarmament talks, calls attention to an outline of the Bible study for the day which is being passed around in mimeographed form. "We're concerned today about how to witness," he says. "Please open your Bibles to Luke 24." There is a rustling of paper as Bibles are opened around the table.

"I'm not coming to you as an expert," Coleman explains. "I'm still learning, still struggling in the Christian life. But I'm excited about sharing Christ and I hope you are, too. Now let's start by looking at the first question of the outline: 'What importance did Jesus give to the Old Testament Scriptures?' "

A dark-haired young woman responds with a statement Jesus made to His disciples. Using *The Living Bible* paraphrase, she reads from Luke 24: "When I was with you before, don't you remember my telling you that everything written about me by Moses and the prophets and in the Psalms must all come true?... Yes, it was written long ago that the Messiah must suffer and die and rise again from the dead on the third day; and that this message of salvation should be taken from Jerusalem to all the nations."

After a brief discussion of the passage, Coleman directs another question. A slender, mustached black responds.

More discussion. Another question and a response. And so it goes until Hackett, the group leader, stands to conclude the session with a short testimony aimed at the ten newcomers:

"For years I was searching. I had a good job here at State and a fine family—our oldest daughter was 'Miss District of Columbia Teenager' in 1969—and yet I was dissatisfied. I hadn't found meaning, an identity for my life. Then, through a Bible study group, I found all this in a personal relationship with Jesus. Now I know where I'm going and what I'm here for.

"About three years ago we started this Bible study. We've seen it grow as more and more people became interested in studying God's Word. If you're here for the first time, we'd like to invite you back, and if you have spiritual questions please talk to me, Chuck Coleman, or any other Christian in our group."

When the closing prayer is given the group does not disperse immediately. Like an extended family, the regulars stay around for a few minutes to get acquainted with newcomers. Both Hackett and Coleman move among the group, greeting old and new friends and responding to questions about the day's study.

At least two more prayer groups meet weekly in State Department conference rooms. One is a women's group coordinated by Sandra Sheskin, an employee who lectures on the Great Seal of the United States to visiting tour groups. "You can really feel the love of Jesus breaking through in our group," she says. "It's especially thrilling to see walls breaking down between black and white."

State's other co-ed group meets on the fifth floor. Ellsworth Donovan, chief of the administrative support division, is involved here along with several other high executives. Of the 9,000 who work in the main building, Donovan has about 1,000 employees in his department. A thirty-one-year government employee, he was a Navy warrant officer in World War II who counseled parents grieving over sons lost in battle. His most remembered case was the Sullivans who lost five sons. "I noticed Mr. Sullivan carrying a Bible, something that stuck in my memory," he recalls. "They seemed to have a deep abiding faith which I didn't have myself at the time."

Donovan remained a nominal church member until 1969. "My wife and I became very discouraged with our church. It was all social-action oriented and didn't even have an adult Sunday school class. One of our sons became friends with a Baptist pastor's son. The minister came to see us and showed us how to have a personal relationship with Christ. After that we became active in his church, Woodlawn Baptist."

Today, in addition to his State Department job, Donovan serves as part-time minister of education for the church and his wife teaches Sunday school. He finds that the fifth-floor Bible study and prayer group at State has helped him become more sensitive in counseling employees. He recalls, for instance, a young woman who was deeply depressed. "We weren't communicating very well until I told her I was a Christian. She said she was a believer, too, and then she really opened up. We got right to the root of her problem and she was able to see the solution. She left with relief written on her face."

Across the Potomac at the mammoth Pentagon, 28,000 military and civilian employees supervise the security and defense of the United States. Within the tiers and corridors of the five-sided building, a veritable city with a basement shopping center, prayer and Bible study groups meet every day.

John Broger, one of the key movers behind the Pentagon groups, is director of the Office of Information and Education for all U.S. armed forces. In this position the mustached, quick-thinking communicator is just two steps down from the Secretary of Defense.

Broger, a former evangelical missionary broadcaster who is now in his forties, knows of seventeen Pentagon groups meeting weekly, plus some twenty military-related home Bible studies associated with the Officers Christian Fellowship. "We print 16,000 cards every month listing the times and places where groups meet within the building. There is a devotional every morning from 7:30 to 8:00 and a chapel each day. Every other Tuesday people at the general and admiral level meet from 6:25 until 8:00 for intensive study in the Word. I myself am involved in a prayer breakfast every Monday morning at the deputy director of defense level."

Another key Pentagon Christian is Colonel Arthur G. Dewey, who directed the prestigious Commission of White House Fellows before taking a sensitive Pentagon assignment in international affairs. Dewey unabashedly testifies that the "new birth works in my life and is working in Washington."

Why such interest in Bible study and prayer groups around the capital? One reason, Dewey thinks is that people tire of being mere spectators in churches. "The groups keep dialogue going. We discover how to be 'doers of the Word' in practical everyday living."

Health, Education, and Welfare stands in sharp contrast to the Pentagon. No groups are known to be operating in the massive HEW bureaucracy.

An evangelical middle-management HEW man, in making a comparison, thinks "military people tend to be more pragmatic, more individual, while here at HEW we have the social planners out to remake society with programs. They don't really feel that praying will accomplish this."

But groups are operative in the National Aeronautics and Space Agency (NASA), the Federal Aviation Agency (FAA), the General Services Administration (GSA), the Supreme Court and many other divisions of government. Because their buildings are clustered close together, FAA, DOT, GSA, and EPA groups combine for occasional noon rallies in a nearby auditorium.

Back on Capitol Hill there are twenty or more prayer and Bible study groups among the 10,000 employees of the legislative branch. These range from a Wednesday breakfast of congressional staffers—administrative and press aides and secretaries—to a group of waiters and waitresses who serve Senators in their private dining rooms. Harold Hughes, when he was still a Senator, reportedly helped serve food to the latter group at their first meeting.

Most of the government employees' groups are similar in several respects. They are relatively unstructured with only rotating voluntary coordinators. They are not tied organizationally to denominations or local churches. Nor are they sponsored by any official government body. Mainline evangelical, with a sprinkling of charismatic neo-Pentecostal participants, they are bound together by a lifeline of spiritual fellowship through prayer, Bible study, and witnessing.

While there are no direct ties to a central coordinating organization, there are key people quietly working behind the scenes to keep things going. Doug Coe's name keeps popping up around the White House and Capitol Hill. The befreckled, dark-haired Coe, a genial man in his forties who bears a resemblance to Gregory Peck, moves easily within high circles, offering personal counsel and encouragement, never involving himself in partisan issues and avoiding reporters like the plague. He may have more influence with high government figures on a personal level than Billy Graham. *Time* calls him the unofficial "real chaplain" of the House and Senate.

Two other Fellowship House associates, Stuart Murdock, a former Pentagon economist, and Fred Hines, an ex-FBI agent, work with lower level government employees on Capitol Hill and within the scattered agencies and cabinet departments.

A fourth "missionary" to government is a personable, red-haired young Californian: Robert L. "Bud" Hancock. Unlike Coe, Murdock, and Hines who work out of Fellowship House, Hancock has a borrowed desk in the Washington offices of the Wycliffe Bible Translators. All four of these government "missionaries" are supported by churches and friends who "believe" in their ministries, though Hancock relies to some extent on consulting fees from Christian missionary organizations.

Hancock came to Washington in 1966 on a State Department educational project, with plans to enter the foreign service. The challenge of inner city ministries, however, led him to accept a job in D.C. mayor Walter Washington's office for two years. "White evangelicals were only tokenly involved," he recalls, "and white liberals were not being received well by the black community. I felt I should try and do something." After the 1968 ghetto riots, Hancock decided to stay on in Washington as a lay missionary to government people.

Hancock lives across the Potomac in Arlington, Virginia, less than fifteen minutes from downtown Washington. One recent Monday morning he left his modest frame house around 6:30, just as his wife, Linda, was rising to get three of four children ready for school. He drove to Fellowship House in a two-year-old Toyota (a gift from a Christian friend) for breakfast and a Bible study led by General M. H. Silverthorn. Afterwards he went to the Wycliffe office to tend to some necessary paperwork and to firm up by telephone a number of appointments throughout the week. At 9:30 he met with a young Christian couple wanting to begin a full-time ministry among inner-city blacks; they wanted advice on raising financial support. At 10:30 he drove to Capitol Hill where he spent an hour counseling a congressional staffer about a personal problem. On this way to an EPA luncheon, he swung by the Department of Treasury building next to the White House to pick up a computer programmer and a policy planner. Both were Christians but worked on different floors. Through Hancock they met for the first time.

At noon the EPA group welcomed Hancock and the visiting brothers from the "Treasury." Hancock himself needed no introduction; he periodically touches base with a number of agency groups; everybody seems to know him. He hoped the Treasury men would get turned on and want to start a group in their building. They listened and were inspired to hear an older woman announce a breakthrough with her son who had a drug problem, and a young scientist say that he and a fellow employee were now working better together because of prayer. The visitors got the idea. They talked with Hancock about starting a group of their own; Hancock volunteered to help them plan the first meeting.

After dropping them off at the Treasury, Hancock returned to southwest Washington for more office visits, more counseling, more listening, more introductions of Christians to fellow believers within the maze of the vast government agencies.

"It's not my job to start new groups," Hancock insists. "The Holy Spirit is a creator, not a duplicator. He merely uses me to bring Christians together. Then they take it from there under His leadership. It's beautiful that way.

"The groups don't belong to anyone. The people in them are just making themselves available to God, having their needs met and discovering their individual missions for him. The dimension of uniqueness among the groups is a tremendous strength for the total body of Christ. It's exciting to look at a map of Washington and to see how groups of believers are meeting and ministering all over the city."

There are some 350,000 white collar workers employed by the Federal government in the Greater Washington area. Their agency bosses are George Wallace's "pointy-headed bureaucrats," the butt of jokes and bitter sarcasm by millions of Americans strapped by high taxes.

The bureaucracy employees spend the money for programs legislated by Congress and authorized by the president—over $300 billion annually. They mail out veterans' and social security checks, mint coins, print postage, regulate interstate commerce, enforce environmental standards, mediate business-labor disputes, maintain a strong defense establishment, keep the machinery of foreign relations lubricated and working, and do a host of other jobs.

For this they are paid better than most Americans and receive up to a month's paid vacation. Median family income in the District of Columbia in the mid-seventies was more than $13,000, higher than any state in the Union. In suburban Montgomery County, Maryland, one of the richest counties in the nation, the median was almost $25,000, with the purchase price of homes averaging more than $50,000. Civil service workers can rarely be dismissed except for gross incompetence, and they can retire on 80 percent of the average highest three years salary. However, executive appointees and congressional staffers—usually paid more than their agency counterparts—are not so secure. They are subject to the whims of politics.

Yet with all the affluence, status, and security that goes with having a job in the capital bureaucracy, government workers still have problems. There are more psychiatrists in the District of Columbia than in any other area in the U.S., 55.6 per 100,000 people, while New York has 25.2, according to A. H. Kumbar, deputy director for Business Affairs for the American Psychiatric Association. (Perhaps this figure should be modified because many, if not most, of the psychiatric patients live in Washington suburbs.) In explanation, Dr. Richard Steinbach, chairman of Georgetown University's Department of Psychiatry, points to the transiency and rootlessness of a great portion of the population which can result in anxieties of loneliness and feelings of separation. The rates of alcoholism, venereal disease, and divorce are higher than most states. Sex-oriented *Playboy* outsells all other magazines on Washington area newsstands (140,000 copies per issue with its raunchy competitor, *Penthouse,* tied with *TV Guide* at 130,000), according to a survey by the *Washington Star-News*[1]. (Nationwide, *Playboy* is number nine and *Reader's Digest* number one.)

Bud Hancock probably understands the problems of government people better than many pastors in the Washington area. "There is an abundance of boredom," he comments. "Many feel no sense of mission or purpose on the job and live only for the weekend. Higher echelon people in particular are susceptible to family crises because of long and demanding job hours and the pressure to keep on the cocktail circuit. Most parties are just chit-chat without opportunity to build meaningful relationships. People caught up in this syndrome are easy marks for alcoholism.

"The forerunner of moral decay is loneliness. Many Washingtonians work in the bureaucracies from nine to 4:30 without close personal ties with any of their fellow employees. They go home to apartment high rises where they do not know their neighbors. Feeling isolated and lonely, they are drawn into a downward moral spiral."

Hancock is a deacon and active with his family in Arlington's Cherrydale Baptist Church. He sees the groups as "supplementing" the ministry of churches by "meeting needs where government people spend one third of their lives before retirement. Through Bible study, prayer, and one-to-one in-depth sharing, significant and lasting relationships can be built on the vertical level with God and on the horizontal with fellow believers."

After years of conducting spiritual growth workshops and helping groups get started, Hancock has developed a credo which he calls "Getting It Together."

> I believe:
> That people are more important than programs.
> That people are persons, not problems.
> That fulfillment through service is a great reward in life.
> That each person is created uniquely and should be so treated.
> That given the opportunity, all people can discover and experience a more meaningful life.
> That continuing relationships are necessary for lasting personal growth.
> That positive action will overcome empty rhetoric and the negative past.
> And that meaning and purpose is found in reconciliation to God through Jesus Christ, the Lord of life.

To realize these ideals, Hancock, like Doug Coe and other Christian lay workers in Washington, encourages deeper involvement in one of the many small, closely knit cell groups that meet for an extended time weekly. These are similar to the weekly Hughes-Colson-Quie-Purcell-Coe cell. Hancock himself meets each Thursday evening for three hours with Colonel Arthur G. Dewey and three others, where they "learn to share" their "lives in pursuit of knowing and loving Christ and knowing and loving one another." Their "principles of agreement," which have been adopted by a number of other cells, include,

> 1. *Commitment.* (a) To one another—a concern for and caring for each other's growth, success and well being. (b) To the priority of meeting weekly.
> 2. *Frankness.* That a spirit of openness be

maintained to yield maximum growth and learning.

3. *Confidentiality*. That what is said of a personal nature in the group stays in the group.

4. *Consensus*. That all actions and decisions are by consensus of the entire group.

5. *Meetings*. That group meetings will be scheduled from 7:30 P.M. and not go later than 10:30.

6. *Visitors*. No visitors. Exception: spouse or fiance on special occasions.

Additionally Hancock and John Broger and other Washingtonians enthusiastic about the potential of the Bible study and prayer meetings and the cell groups are promoting a unique plan to involve additional people beyond the several thousand already participating in Washington. Their basic idea for extension comes from a pilot "hot line" program which Broger devised for getting military personnel with problems into contact with trained peer counselors.

The Christian leaders have begun broadcasting radio announcements over Washington stations asking, "Are you a Christian who needs fellowship at work? Call_____and give us your phone number. We will put you in touch with other Christians in your department."

Another spot invites listeners desiring Christian counseling to call; the aim is to put them in touch with trained counselors within their own departments. Training is offered in a class at the Pentagon; other classes are planned.

In a "rationale" for the program, Broger says:

> There is rarely an agency, an office building, an apartment building, business, school, or neighborhood where Christians cannot be found. Yet, very few Christians side by side know each other or know that they share a common faith in Christ.
>
> The need to be stimulated to find answers to life's questions in the Bible, the need for peer-level fellowship and encouragement, the need for

someone to listen and offer counsel, the need for someone who cares about my success and well-being, the need for involvement according to my interests, skills and goals, and the need for courage to be a witness for my Lord—all these and many more are real needs. Through discovering one another where God has placed us, these needs can be met, making a new sense of mission and purpose possible.[2]

This innovative program called "LINK," complete with plans for city-wide implementation, was introduced by Broger to the National Association of Evangelicals annual meeting in April, 1974. Pioneered by Christians in Washington, it could become a model for other cities across the land—the means by which much of America experiences the healing, life-uplifting touch of Christians who care.

CHAPTER FIVE

Abram's Embassy

Long-time observers of the Washington religious scene see on it the long shadow of a man who died in 1969 at age 83: Abraham "Abram" Vereide. They remember him as the broad-shouldered, ramrod-straight, white-haired Norwegian immigrant who founded International Christian Leadership.

"His commitment over a period of thirty years stimulated everything that is going on around here," declares Harold Hughes.

That may be an over-statement, but at the mention of Abram Vereide's name, some veteran power figures in Washington lower their voices and recall almost reverently their associations with him. "He was like an older brother to me," states Rep. Charles Bennett (D. Fla.), who initiated landmark ethics bills in Congress. "He always gave the impression that he wanted to walk beside you and not in front of you," says West Virginia's Senator Jennings Randolph in underscoring Vereide's genuine, no-hidden-agenda interest in the lawmakers as individuals rather than as people to be manipulated.

The breakfast prayer groups founded by Vereide, asserts Senator Stuart Symington (D.-Mo.), have done "more for me than anything else since I came to Washington." Symington lost his childhood faith during college years and did not attend church until an act of rededication he attributes to the Wednesday morning Senate prayer session.

Richard Halverson, the senior minister at Fourth

81

Presbyterian Church who for years was associated with Vereide, says the Norwegian's life and work were propelled by Second Corinthians 5:18: "[God] has given to us the ministry of reconciliation." Halverson describes him as a man for all seasons:

"Abram had a strange natural sense that transcended all the divisions that separate men. Not that he was bigger than other people, but in his thinking he found intolerable any lines of demarcation between people. He saw the church as a universal fellowship, and he was incapable of recognizing ecclesiastical divisions in that fellowship. He was as free with Catholic Christians as with Protestant Christians. Some evangelicals criticized him for this inclusivism. But liberals criticized him, too; they thought he was too evangelical in theology, and they disliked his emphasis on evangelism. In all the meetings where he had occasion to speak he invariably gave centrality to Christ.

"He could see a little cell in every department of government sending out healthy, renewing vibrations. It never happened in his lifetime, but it's happening now, and it's something I marvel at."

Vereide's vision did not begin in Washington. The roots of his deep, mystical faith go back to his Lutheran childhood in Norway. He was only eight years old when his mother died. Crushed with sorrow and "indescribable loneliness," he ran into a thicket of elder trees and threw himself on the ground. While weeping and praying he suddenly had a "vivid consciousness of a Divine Presence," followed by a "sense of release, of peace and joy."

Ten years later he was a strong-muscled, keen-minded sensitive youth ready for college but without funds for tuition. Frustrated, he was walking behind a plow when "the sense of God came vividly to me, with the arresting question, 'What are you going to do with your life?' " He reined in the horse and knelt on the upturned sod. Again, he recalled later, "God spoke and the fellowship with the Unseen became particularly real."

At the time, thousands of Europeans were emigrating to America and writing back home that it was indeed a land where opportunity abounded. Veriede began to wonder whether at least part of his future might lie there. Within a year he was offered a steamship ticket to America by a family friend who had purchased it and then decided not to go. He took it.

Upon arrival at the immigration center on Ellis Island in New York harbor in 1905, he was handed a gift New Testament by a smiling woman. "This book is the foundation of America and the secret of its greatness and strength," she said. The young Norwegian never forgot the incident.

His only contact was the name of a man who lived in Montana. The name had been given him by an immigration promoter. It took all his savings to make the trip to the then rough and rowdy northwest. The Butte contact turned out to be a wild-west character who lived in a shack at the edge of town; he knew every saloon and bawdy house for miles around.

Disillusioned, but buoyed by a fresh "sense of the Divine Presence," young Vereide moved on. Eventually he met a family of Norwegian background in Butte. The family took him to their Methodist church where he struck up a friendship with the pastor, N. L. Hansen, who was also the denominational superintendent. Over the ensuing months, Pastor Hansen tutored Vereide in evangelical theology, then gave him a preaching license and a parish of lumberjacks and homesteaders near Great Falls.

The young Norwegian, making his pastoral rounds on horseback, loved his work but he became convinced he needed more formal training. He enrolled in Northwestern University at Evanston, Illinois. For two years he attended classes both at the university and at the adjoining Garrett (Methodist) seminary. Then he fell ill with tuberculosis and had to leave school.

Vereide returned to Montana and in time recovered. He married Pastor Hansen's oldest daughter Mattie in 1910. Afterward came Methodist pastorates in Spokane, Washington, and Portland, Oregon, where he gained prominence as a preacher and attention for his work with immigrants.

In 1916 he was transferred to First Methodist Church in Seattle, the most important church in the conference. Immigrants were then pouring into the port city. Knowing from personal experience their problems of adjustment, Vereide mobilized his church to help them. He established homes for girls, men, and delinquents, an employment office, tutoring services, and Americanization classes. The immigrants could see in Vereide one of their own kind who had fallen in love with his adopted country. At times he burst into tears when talking about America; they could see he was sometimes stirred at the mere sight of a flag. He commented later: "The passion of my life at that time was to win immigrants to Christ and help them to become real assets as industrious and patriotic citizens."

His relief work in Seattle won him the community's respect. Seven years after his arrival civic leaders sent him on a three-month fact-finding mission across the country to determine the most effective ways to cope with certain social needs. This led to the establishment of a local unit of Good Will Industries, a turn-waste-into-wages movement started in the twenties by a Methodist minister in Boston. (The movement, a nondenominational one combining industrial relief with training of the handicapped and other social service, later jelled into Goodwill Industries of America.) For nine years Vereide headed up Good Will and, with the help of assistants, carried out his pastoral duties at First Methodist.

In 1931 Vereide left for Boston to become associate general superintendent of Goodwill Industries of America. As he grappled with the economic and social conditions of the Depression and consulted with political and industrial leaders, he concluded it would take changed men to change society. A turning-point was a conference New York governor Franklin D. Roosevelt arranged for him with James Farrell, president of United States Steel Corporation. Farrell told Vereide that the depressions of America had been preceded by spiritual decline while rejuvenation socially and economically followed spiritual renewal.

"I'm a Catholic, and we don't go in much for revivals and such things," said Farrell, "but I'm sure that if we don't get a thorough revival of genuine religion, with confession of our sins and repentance toward God by high and low, and a return to prayer and the Bible, we are headed for chaos. It must come through laymen, and the leaders of industry and business must begin to lead." Vereide never forgot those words.

A few weeks later Vereide was speaking for Goodwill in Detroit. The wife of Henry Ford I was in the audience. Impressed, she arranged for her husband to meet the Norwegian. After several office visits, Ford invited Vereide to spend two days with him alone in Sudbury, Massachusetts. Vereide found Ford "befuddled" from studying Hindu mysticism and other religious and philosophical ideas but managed to engage him in serious Bible study. After this time together and several subsequent meetings back in Michigan, Ford announced: "Vereide, I've got it! I found the release you spoke of. I've made my surrender. The only thing that matters is God's will. I'm anchored in Jesus Christ."

Vereide left Goodwill to become a traveling lecturer and evangelist, serving for a few months in 1934 as evangelism director for the San Francisco Council of Churches. In San Francisco he met with a group of executives for prayer and Bible study at the Pacific Union Club. These meetings convinced him that the way to reach the kind of people he wanted to reach had to be outside the usual church channels: in gatherings of peers, where discussions could be informal and uninhibited. San Francisco became the foundation for Vereide's future work.

Vereide returned to Seattle, making it the base for his itinerant ministry. In the mid-thirties he wrote that he had become "heartsick" over the nation's spiritual condition. The politicians he met seemed "unfit for leadership." He worried about "leftist subversives" maneuvering for control.

While praying and pondering over the situation, he ran into an old acquaintance, merchant Walter Douglass, a Seattle business leader. Douglass agreed with Vereide that the country was going to the dogs but challenged the Norwegian to "get after fellows like me." Douglass also offered to stake Vereide if he would work with the leaders and other influential men of the city. William St. Clair, the president of the largest department store in the northwest, also offered support, and he drew up a list of nineteen executives to invite to a Thursday breakfast meeting.

Of those who gathered that Thursday in April, 1935, only one said he was active in a church but he confessed he was a hypocrite. At Vereide's suggestion they met the following week—and the week after that—to study the Bible and apply its teachings to private and business life. The breakfast meetings, marked by candid sharing, continued regularly and became known as "City Chapel," with a number of Seattle's business leaders committing their lives to Christ. The moral climate at the city's highest levels began changing. A labor leader who had led a crippling strike and his chief industry opponent were reconciled and became close friends.

One of the City Chapel members, Arthur Langlie, was elected governor of the state in 1939. Vereide helped him plan a prayer breakfast. It was held the day Langlie took office, and some 300 leaders of both political parties attended. The Chief Justice read Scripture. A Republican and a Democrat both prayed. Governor Langlie himself told how he had become a follower of Christ. Then all joined in the Lord's Prayer and concluded by singing, "My Country, 'Tis of Thee."

In time, the prayer breakfast idea caught on across the nation. Leaders from New York, Chicago, Boston, Baltimore, and Washington, D. C., asked Vereide to come. It was inevitable that he would give special attention to Washington, where national leadership was concentrated. On a visit in the fall of 1941 he began systematically calling on members of Congress and other capital notables. Then came Pearl Harbor. In January, 1942, some eighty members of Congress and other political leaders, worried by the new war, braved a heavy snowfall and gathered at the old Willard Hotel on Pennsylvania Avenue for the capital's first prayer breakfast.

Francis Sayre, the recently returned high commissioner to the Philippines, presided. Howard B. Coonley, president of the National Association of Manufacturers, gave a message. Then Vereide told the story of the breakfast groups. He challenged the congressmen to set the example for national life and begin meeting regularly for prayer and Bible study. He concluded with a quote from William Penn: "Men must either be governed by God or ruled by tyrants."

At this point in the historical record there is disagreement over exactly how the House and Senate prayer breakfasts originated. A brochure published by Vereide's organization in the fifties states that weekly breakfast groups were formed in both houses of Congress as a result of Vereide's suggestion at the Willard Hotel meeting. This contention is supported in a biography of Vereide by his friend Norman Grubb. "Breakfast" may be the key word.

One of the men at the Willard meeting was Congressman Frank Carlson of Kansas. (Carlson, who attended Washington's First Baptist Church, became governor of Kansas in 1946 after serving six terms in Congress. In 1949 he chaired the National Governors' Conference. He served in the Senate from 1950 to 1969 and was for years president of International Christian Leadership.) According to Carlson, the Senate prayer group had its beginnings on the morning after Pearl Harbor when editor-publisher David Lawrence (*U.S. News and World Report*) and three senators decided they could at least pray about the national tragedy. They slipped into an empty room on the Senate side of the Capitol and prayed. In the next weeks they met several more times. Following the Willard meeting they shifted to a Wednesday morning breakfast session in the Vandenburg Room of the Senate restaurant, with Senator Alexander Wiley of Wisconsin emerging as the key leader. In the years since then leadership and membership have changed, of course, but the time and place have not.

The House prayer group did not begin until early 1943, according to Dr. Walter H. Judd. A former Congregational medical missionary to China and a ten-term Minnesota congressman, Judd says it all began "sort of spontaneously" right in his office. He, Brooks Hays of Arkansas, Percy Priest of Tennessee, John Murdock of Arizona, Paul Cunningham of Iowa, and several others decided to meet on Thursday mornings for prayer. At that time, Judd had not yet met Vereide.

Nearly a year later, says Judd, Vereide persuaded several of the group's members to switch the prayer meeting to a breakfast format.

"That nearly killed us," asserts Judd. "We met in a corner of a cafeteria. It was noisy. People stared while we prayed. Some wondered whether we were interested in calling on God or in getting kudos. The group started going downhill. Vereide was always inviting outsiders in—visiting ministers and others. There was too much exhibition and inhibition. It was becoming just another formality. I dropped out. Finally the group was able to get a private dining room in the Senate, and the members voted to keep outsiders out. That saved it. A number of us started attending again."

Meanwhile, Vereide and his family in 1943 moved from Seattle to Chicago, where he incorporated his ministry as the National Committee for Christian Leadership, which later became International Christian Leadership (ICL). They moved to Washington the following year, and Vereide began building a core of leaders to help with the work. The new ICL board sponsored a prayer breakfast at the 1944 Republican convention. The board members were Congressmen Judd, Hays, and John Sparkman of Alabama; Senators Wiley and Raymond E. Willis; editor Lawrence (a Jew who felt quite at home in Christian circles); and retired admiral C. S. Freeman.

Something else was needed—a center where Christian leaders could meet in privacy for prayer and serious discussion without fear of reading about it in the newspaper the next morning. Vereide thought the answer might be a "fellowship house," similar to Calvary House operated by his Episcopal rector friend Sam Shoemaker in New York. As a frequent visitor to Calvary House, Vereide had been impressed by how lives had been changed in prayer groups and conferences at the house.

Such a house already existed in Washington. Marian Johnson, a widowed second cousin of Franklin D. Roosevelt and a convert from Calvary House, had rented a spacious residence on Massachusetts Avenue in 1942 and invited Christian leaders to make it a center for fellowship. Vereide obtained permission for his group to meet there. A few months later, however, the house was sold, and Vereide became convinced the ICL needed to buy a house of its own. The board members were willing—provided the money could be raised. Vereide located a large four-story residence for sale on Embassy Row, next to the Korean embassy on Massachusetts Avenue's Sheridan Circle. One of his acquaintances, hearing of the need and opportunity, wrote a check for $50,000, which Vereide promptly plunked down as down payment. The wife of the man who wrote the check, though, stopped payment on it, and—with the board members suddenly disinterested—Vereide was left on his own.

"It was one of the very difficult times in Abram's life," says Halverson, "but he and Mattie persevered, and they were able to keep the house."

Vereide set up the Fellowship House Foundation to handle legal and financial affairs, staked out an apartment on the top floor for his family, and threw open the doors to his "Christian embassy"—as he called it—to the ministry of reaching and nurturing the nation's leaders for Christ.

With the war's end came the organization of the United Nations in San Francisco. Vereide was there to meet Christian leaders from abroad. In 1946 he went overseas himself to meet lay leaders in other countries who also knew and followed Christ. During an international peace conference in Paris he conducted daily prayer meetings in the apartment of U. S. delegate Arthur Vandenberg.

As the prayer-breakfast idea spread globally in succeeding years the name International Council for Christian Leadership was used for a time to denote ICL's overseas work. ICL's goal was reflected in a motto of sorts: "Every Christian a leader, every leader a Christian." One of the early information pamphlets describes ICL as "an informal association of concerned laymen banded together to find through Christ the better way of everyday living and to promote for home, community, nation, and world a more effective Christian leadership."

Seven "challenging practices" were encouraged as a program for self-development. The first was: "To check our lives frequently against God's Word and purpose for us, to admit promptly our faults, to seek God's forgiveness, and to accept it gratefully in Christ's name, making whatever restitution seems right in particular instances." Others involved maintaining a private devotional life, being active in a church, witnessing, giving time and money to God's work, participating in group meetings, and endeavoring "to meet every problem, relationship, temptation, and opportunity in a Christlike manner with God's help, refusing any compromise in the application of the basic spiritual imperatives in the teachings of Christ."

Vereide and his colleagues preferred not to think of ICL as an organization but as a fellowship that embraced Christian leaders throughout the world—whether they knew it or not. To Vereide, even the Pope and Billy Graham were members. (Graham and other evangelical notables were friends of Vereide and they sometimes took part in ICL activities, but they didn't see ICL in quite the same all-embracing way he did.) Despite his view of ICL as a noninstitution, Vereide applied organizational methods and structures to the work, and in the public eye ICL was seen as but one of many Christian outreach organizations.

Washington, nerve center of America and a major crossroads of world power, was the ideal headquarters city for ICL. From here, Vereide reasoned, the world quite literally could be reached for Christ.

Vereide's Washington "parish" included the House and Senate, where he was looked on as an unofficial but valued chaplain. He was the pastor-confidant of many key government leaders who knew he could be trusted to keep confidences from gossip-scouting columnists and political opponents. In his dealings with government officials he observed the ground rules laid down by the congressional prayer groups: no partisan politics, denominationalism, or financial appeals. He kept a low profile. Newspapers rarely mentioned his name. Yet, according to authoritative observers, he was one of the most influential men in the capital.

His visits to government offices were brief but memorable. In contrast to most other callers who would come asking favors, Vereide wanted nothing but to listen, encourage, and offer a promise from Scripture. After a five- or ten-minute exchange, he would put an arm around the man with whom he was speaking and break into prayer. Some who experienced the Vereide touch say it was like standing shoulder to shoulder with God. Senator Ralph Flanders of Vermont said that whenever Vereide stopped by for a visit, "I dropped everything and expected a message from the Lord." His poise, says Richard Halverson, "was a gift of God."

Douglas Coe, one of his closest associates, tells the story of how Vereide one day dropped in to see the D. C. mayor. Told that the mayor was in a meeting with his council and could not be disturbed, Vereide located the meeting room and walked in as if he belonged there. He told those assembled of his concern and love for them and suggested they should sponsor a District of Columbia prayer breakfast. When several politely nodded agreement he scheduled a date on the spot. Such breakfasts are still a part of District public life.

Another time, just after John F. Kennedy was elected President but before the inauguration, Vereide on a visit to the Senate spotted Kennedy surrounded by a large group of friends, aides, and Secret Service personnel. The venerable Norwegian pushed his way through the crowd, put both hands on Kennedy's shoulders, looked him square in the eye, then prayed for him.

Vereide's forte was dialogue with four or five men at a time over a meal. He would get them talking about problems of the nation, expressing viewpoints which might be beyond his depth, then at just the right moment perhaps ask, "What is the greatest discovery you have made this week?" This would lead into conversation about Jesus and the wisdom he offered.

While Vereide was no doctrinal hair-splitting Bible scholar, he did have theological convictions. A staunch evangelical conservative who traveled the middle of the road, he believed the Bible to be God's Word for all classes, occupations, and cultures, Jesus to be the divine Son of God who brings new life and joy to those who receive Him as Savior and Lord, and love to be the hallmark of life. Love, he said, is "the capacity to understand ... and redemptively help all people."

Long before small interaction groups became a popular

style pushed by the denominations, Vereide decided they were the best vehicle for promoting effective Christian leadership. He felt that each vocational segment of urban society—education, business, industry, the professions, labor, government—needed a group where people could meet weekly to "check their operations with the divine blueprint and invoke the guidance and blessing of God as they seek His solution to current problems." These groups, with one or more committed individuals at the core, would complement the churches, not compete with them. Every city, he believed, was "teeming with hungry, groping men, desperately in need of God," many of whom seldom if ever attended a church.

(In their early years in Washington, Vereide and his family usually attended National Presbyterian Church or the Presbyterian Church of the Pilgrims. Later on they often attended Fourth Presbyterian. But, says Halverson, "Abram felt he was a part of every church in the city.")

"Everywhere and all the time, you and I are the representatives of Jesus Christ," Vereide told his prayer-group members, and he practiced what he preached. Getting into a cab, he inevitably would steer the driver into a conversation about spiritual issues, offering encouragement where he sensed a need, often trying to lead him to make a definite decision for Christ. He saw every person he met—the delivery man, the mailman, the service station attendant, the hotel maid—as someone whom he might introduce to Christ, not as so many spiritual scalps to collect, but as persons who in the depths of their being were hungering after God.

He drew every member of his family into the ICL work. Wife Mattie kept the books and served as hostess at Fellowship House, cooking and serving guests even after she was crippled by a stroke. Oldest son, Warren, worked for the State Department and later became Safety Engineer for the city of Seattle where he promoted breakfast groups among his father's old friends. The two younger sons, Milton and Abraham, Jr., also boosted ICL, with Milton going as a Presbyterian missionary to the Philippines. Daughter Alicia, a Pentecostal preacher, was widowed in 1942 and joined her parents in Washington in 1946. Helping her mother in the household chores and with hostess work at first, she soon became to the wives of senators and congressmen and others what her father was to the men. She started the Congressional Wives Prayer Luncheon (see chapter ten), prayer groups for women in the Library of Congress and the Pentagon, and a group for wives of diplomats.

Throughout the fifties Vereide was constantly on the go, both in America and abroad, everywhere quietly pushing the ICL concept. He moved with ease among corporate czars and foreign royalty, and displayed an adroitness at building rapport with men not his kind. Whether they were Catholic, Christian Scientist, agnostic, Buddhist, or whatever, Vereide believed God had a word for each.

The first Presidential Prayer Breakfast was held in 1953, at the outset of the new Eisenhower administration. Frank Carlson, by this time a senator and the man who managed Dwight Eisenhower's campaign, was the prime mover behind the breakfast. After Ike's election, Carlson thought it would be good to get the House and Senate together for a prayer breakfast and to invite the new President. Logistics, however, seemed formidable. Then Carlson remembered that hotel magnate Conrad Hilton owed him a favor. Hilton had wanted to meet Billy Graham, and Carlson had gotten the two together in Denver. The grateful Hilton thanked the senator and invited him to call if special help were ever needed.

Carlson arranged for Hilton to host the breakfast at the Mayflower Hotel. The proceedings were recorded by a White House stenographer and inserted into the February 10, 1953, *Congressional Record.* About 500 persons attended, among them a large number of Senate and House members, justices of the Supreme Court, Cabinet and White House officials, Vice President Richard Nixon, and President Eisenhower. Carlson, president of ICL, presided. Rep. Katherine St. George (D.-N.Y.) led in the opening prayer and read a Scripture passage. Vereide offered a dedicatory prayer for the new cabinet members. Ike himself gave a brief message. Beneath a picture of Uncle Sam kneeling, he declared that prayer is "simply a necessity" for government leaders. Afterward, Chief Justice Frederick Vinson of the Supreme

Court, told Billy Graham he'd "never seen anything like this meeting in all my years here in Washington."

ICL leaders were a little nervous about the press attention given to the breakfast, partly because of church-state implications, partly out of concern for everybody's privacy, especially Eisenhower's.

Before his inauguration Eisenhower and his wife Mamie had been attending membership classes at the National Presbyterian Church. On the morning of the inauguration the Eisenhower family attended a precedent-breaking pre-inaugural service at the church. After the service, Ike returned to his hotel suite and wrote the prayer he read at the inaugural ceremonies—another first.

Two weeks later the Eisenhowers joined National Presbyterian. In accordance with membership conditions, Ike—raised in the River Brethren Church, where infant baptism was not practiced—was baptized and confirmed, another historical first. He explained later that he had not been baptized or joined a church previously because he had not lived in one place long enough. White House correspondent Forrest Boyd of Mutual radio network points out in his book *Instant Analysis* that the baptism service was supposed to have been private, but news leaked out. Ike's press secretary claimed later that the officiating minister, Dr. Edward L. R. Elson, had been asked not to give out a press release. According to Boyd, a wire service reporter spotted on a desk in the church office a printed statement about the baptism and broke the story. Elson explained he had prepared the statement only to insure that Presbyterian language was used correctly in subsequent news stories.

Ike was reportedly upset over the publicity, and all the more when Senator Matthew Neely of West Virginia charged that the President's new church affiliation had been politically inspired. Some reporters, Boyd notes, "had the impression that [Ike] was so irritated he was tempted to quit going to the National Presbyterian Church almost before he started."

The storm blew over, though, and Ike seemed to enjoy the prayer breakfast, which became an annual event. At the 1956 Presidential Prayer Breakfast Conrad Hilton presented to him the desk on which he had written his inaugural prayer. Reminiscing about that prayer, Ike told the breakfast audience it "seemed to me a perfectly natural thing to do.... I know very few ... who tell me they are atheists or agnostics. But we find among the laity a curious diffidence in merely stating the fact that they believe there is a God and that He is more powerful than they and that they depend on Him.... I think that [inaugural] prayer is somewhat related to these prayer breakfasts. We can pray in our quarters, but we can come to gatherings occasionally ... announcing to the world ... that this nation is still a nation under God."

As participation in the annual event broadened, and to avoid focusing excessive attention on the President (the point, after all, was to get people's minds on God), the name was changed to the National Prayer Breakfast.

The first ICL Governor's Prayer Breakfast was hosted by former U.S. Senator Price Daniel on the day of his inauguration as governor of Texas. Many governors have held similar events annually since then. Daniel had been an ICL board member and a leader of the Senate prayer group. "While I was a member of the Senate," he commented, "nothing encouraged or inspired or sustained me more than the weekly meetings at the prayer breakfast."

Over the years a number of full-time workers became associated with ICL. Vereide's first administrative assistant was Waldron Scott, a staffer with the Colorado-based Navigators outreach ministry. (Scott went on to become an executive leader of the Navigators. In late 1974 he became International Administrator of the World Evangelical Fellowship.) ICL's first overseas worker was Wesleyan evangelist Wallace Haines. In 1950 Vereide asked Haines to go to Europe, to find out "what God is doing, and relate to it." Haines moved his family to Paris, organized an ICL council, and carried the breakfast group idea into other European countries. Now based in suburban London, he is still involved in the same ministry (minus the ICL name)—the senior veteran in the work begun by Vereide.

In 1956, after three years of coaxing by Vereide, Richard Halverson accepted a post as ICL associate executive director.

Halverson had been a minister-at-large with the big Hollywood Presbyterian Church in California. He worked under Vereide for two years, then in 1958 became pastor of Washington's Fourth Presbyterian Church (now located across the District line in Bethesda, Maryland). He continued to maintain close ties with Vereide, serving in a leadership role on ICL's board.

In 1959 Douglas Coe became Vereide's executive assistant. Halverson had met him on a visit to Willamette University in Salem, Oregon, where Coe was serving with the Navigators. At the university, Coe had been the spiritual confidant of a young political science professor named Mark Hatfield, the Inter-Varsity Christian Fellowship faculty advisor who would later come to Washington as a senator and become deeply involved with ICL. Coe was a disciple of the late Navigators founder Dawson Trotman, who emphasized reaching persons one at a time for Christ and building long-term relationships with them. Service with the Navigators thus was good preparation for ICL's kind of work. Coe fit in well at ICL and soon was assigned prime leadership responsibilities. Much more reserved than the aggressive Vereide, he chose to work quietly behind the scenes but nonetheless established many influential contacts and fast friendships with high government people. After Vereide's death he became ICL's executive director, working closely with Halverson and other board members and staffers to accomplish the work begun by the Norwegian immigrant. (Coe applies the Trotman touch in more ways than one: he uses Trotman's old putter exclusively on golf greens.)

The paid staff workers, supported by gifts from churches and friends, are only part of the story. Indeed, says Halverson, "99 percent of Abram's vision has been carried on by lay people." Many lay persons have been associated with the work over the years. ICL board presidents included Boyd Leedom, chairman of the National Labor Relations Board, and George Hayes, black head of the D. C. Public Utilities Commission, both deceased. Among other leaders are retired Marine general M. H. Silverthorn, utilities contractor Winston Weaver, and attorney James Bell.

Silverthorn, assistant director of the Office of Defense Mobilization under President Eisenhower after retiring from the Marines, was invited by a friend to the national Presidential Prayer Breakfast in 1957. A few weeks later he visited with Vereide and discovered "Abram was in the kind of work I wanted to do myself." Vereide assigned him some tasks, and that summer he resigned his ODM job to run the ICL office on a volunteer basis. The aging Silverthorne—who spent most of his life in Navy chapels and eschews denominational labels—subsequently became a member of ICL's executive committee, and he still serves the ministry in an advisory capacity.

Weaver, a Mennonite who lives in Harrisonburg, Virginia, was introduced to ICL in 1960 when a Washington power company vice-president took him to an ICL luncheon for executives. Weaver returned on his own the following week and met Vereide. "The only ability God requires is availability," he remembers Vereide saying. That day Weaver made himself available to God—and ICL. For ten years beginning in 1961 he got up at four A.M. every Tuesday to drive the 130 miles from Harrisonburg to Washington to attend the weekly 7:15 A.M. ICL strategy and policy-making sessions. He became vice-president of the executive committee. As a member of the present-day ministry's "core group"—the equivalent of the executive committee—he often makes the trip two or three times a week. In 1974 he was appointed liaison person for the White House executive-level prayer group, relieving Coe of that duty.

Bell is the senior member of a Washington law firm (a chief client is Pan American World Airways). He first met Vereide in 1952 when a friend invited him to a dinner at Fellowship House. An Episcopalian converted three years earlier under the preaching of British evangelist Brian Green, Bell says he became ICL's "Martha in the kitchen" in legal affairs, gradually getting involved in other phases of the work. Today he is president of the core group.

Beneath the involvement of these and other workers in the Washington ministry is the initial impact Vereide made on their lives. "I can't begin to describe how much he meant to my wife and me," says Weaver. "He cared about people, and he trusted everybody. He had faith in us, and he made us *want* to live up to our commitment to Christ."

Vereide was not without faults. In a sense, says Halverson, the Norwegian was a loner. Sometimes he went ahead with an idea despite opposition by the board or executive committee. But there was no bitterness or dissension. "He was loved and revered to a fault," comments Halverson, "hence got away with it—often to the frustration of his associates who had to implement even a bad idea." Vereide also disliked dealing with negative aspects of the work such as disciplining a worker or terminating an employee. Somebody else always had to handle these matters. He declined to be critical toward anyone, a seeming virtue, but it meant that those around him had to pick up the pieces when things went sour. "He lived so completely in his vision that failure was unknown to him," asserts Halverson. "A plan could fall apart, and he would move ahead as though it hadn't happened. This was fine in a way, but it meant often that we did not learn from our mistakes."

Vereide had suffered a heart attack in 1953, the year of the first Presidential Prayer Breakfast, but he kept going. During the 1960s, however, friends could see he was going downhill physically. Toward the end Halverson and the others spent a lot of time with him, probing his mind, much like disciples in ancient times. "We didn't idolize him," states Halverson. "We loved him as an elder brother, and we wanted to know how his work might best be continued."

The last week of Vereide's life—his 83rd year—began on a Sunday in May 1969, when he flew to Louisiana to participate in the Governor's Prayer Breakfast there. On the plane he sat beside a senator's daughter. During a conversation he urged her—as he had so many others before—to accept Christ, to experience the new life in Him. He returned to his retirement-village apartment near Washington on Wednesday and in the evening hosted a Fellowship House dinner for a newly appointed ambassador. (The old Fellowship House had been sold in 1963 and a large new residence purchased on a secluded street near the Shoreham

Hotel, a bit further out in the northwest part of town.)

On the following evening he hosted a dinner for close friends and took part in a women's-group planning meeting. Friday he went to Capitol Hill for lunch. That night at his apartment he got out of bed to get a drink of water and collapsed in the kitchen. God had called His ambassador home.

Billy Graham observed in memoriam: "Abraham Vereide contributed more to encourage spiritual leadership than any man I know."

Mattie had preceded her husband in death by several months, and their daughter Alicia died in 1972. (Women as well as men have been active in both staff and volunteer roles in the ministry begun by Vereide. Among these are Alicia's daughter Marlene, Marian Johnson [the Roosevelt cousin mentioned earlier], staffer Barbara Priddy [a former Young Life worker in California], and dozens of others.)

In an effort to deinstitutionalize the work, International Christian Leadership was formally disbanded as a corporate entity in 1971. "We want to keep attention off organization and on Christ," explains Coe. Members now refer to the ministry simply as "the fellowship." Fellowship Foundation trustees look after property and legal matters, and the core group handles coordination and decision-making when needed. Halverson defines the core as "a fellowship of brothers who seek consensus."

Both professional and volunteer workers are known as "associates." Former associate John Curry, a physician, describes the associates as "people with a calling in life to make contact with other people," following the example of Vereide who was forever "drawing a circle that included someone else." Those contacted, he says, are brought together in a group where they ask God what He wants them to be and do. "Once the group is formed we have no control over it. Nor do we know what God is calling individual disciples to do. He may want them to work with prisoners, senators, military men at the Pentagon, embassy personnel, American Indians, or some other group. We only know He is calling them to do something." It is a matter, adds Coe, of the Holy Spirit leading people "to do their own thing for Christ."

Among the reminders of Vereide at Fellowship House is a portrait overlooking the expansive, well-appointed living room. Here groups of several dozen or so at a time gather for prayer, Bible study, and discussion. Smaller cell groups huddle in alcoves and other rooms. Breakfast, luncheon, and dinner groups assemble around an enormous table in the chandeliered dining room. Another reminder is the elegant Vereide Memorial Library room.

Fellowship House was Vereide's home, not a headquarters for an organization, Coe points out. Vereide's example inspired a number of others across America to use their homes in the same way. To his "family" of spiritual brothers and sisters in Washington, linked by love and purpose, Fellowship House is still a home. A few of them live there, some temporarily, some more or less permanently, usually with a married couple overseeing the household and acting as host and hostess for the hundreds who come for meetings and meals. "We never advertise," said Dr. Curry cautiously when he and his wife were living there. "Guests are invited by friends, and they include a sizable percentage of internationals." Publicity, he added, "gives us the heebie jeebies. We don't want to become a landmark for Christian tourists."

Thus the "embassy" Vereide established remains, and his work endures. He personally influenced thousands of community, national, and world leaders, who in turn have influenced countless others, a remarkable chain reaction of one life touching another that continues to this day. Many of them have never heard of Vereide, much less seen him. Yet his shadow is upon them.

CHAPTER SIX

Christians in the Senate

Abraham Vereide's ideal of Christian brotherhood among partisan politicians was dramatically demonstrated on Friday night January 30, 1973.

Democratic Senator John Stennis was shot twice by robbers on the sidewalk in front of his Washington home. Critically wounded, he was rushed to Walter Reed Hospital where some doctors did not expect him to live.

Upon hearing the news, Stennis's Republican colleague Mark Hatfield—his oft-time opponent on military expenditures and civil rights—rushed to the hospital. As the Mississippi legislator lay near death, Hatfield remained near his side through the night, maintaining a prayer vigil and answering the telephone.

The next morning the Senate prayer group met as usual. Republicans and Democrats, conservatives and liberals, they joined hands and prayed for "Brother John."

The following day was the date for the National Prayer Breakfast at which Stennis was to have presided. Rep. Albert Quie, a member of the House of Representatives prayer group, took his place. Quie and Hatfield requested prayer for Stennis, who was still on the critical list.

The Senate and House prayer groups and other groups across Washington prayed for him regularly. In the weeks that followed, Stennis slowly rallied from the brink of the grave. The next year he was back to chair the National Prayer

Breakfast and express thanks. "Prayers were my rallying point," he declared with deep emotion. "The chief surgeon told me, 'a High Hand entered your case.' "

Stennis and Hatfield, who in many ways are complete opposites, belong to what has been called the "world's most exclusive club." With only 100 members, the United States Senate wields enormous power. Besides voting on bills which the House of Representatives usually originates, the Senate has certain exclusive powers assigned by the constitution: approval of treaties and presidential appointments, and the sole right to conduct an impeachment trial of the president.

Senators are elected two to a state for six-year terms, whereas House members are chosen from population districts of about 500,000 every two years. Sparsely populated Wyoming, for example, has one congressman and two senators while New York has forty-three members in the House, yet still just two senators. This lopsided arrangement was inserted in the constitution to persuade smaller states to come into the Union.

By virtue of their longer terms, senators find it easier to build a strong power base than do most House members. Some have remained in office for decades, gaining the strength from seniority that has led to chairmanships of influential committees. The cartoon caricature of a frock-coated, bespectacled, white-maned character wearing a string bow-tie is at least partly true, for senators are young at sixty—especially southerners.

Stennis, for example, is in his seventies and has served since 1947, yet he is the *junior* senator from Mississippi. As chairman of the powerful Senate Armed Services Committee, no new military program of consequence can be launched without his consent.

The Senate chamber bears hoary symbols of God and country. Every session is opened with prayer by the official chaplain. The motto *Annuit Coeptis* (God Has Favored Our Undertakings) is sculptured over the east entrance. *Novus Ordo Seclorum* (A New Order of the Ages) and "In God We Trust" crown the west and south doorways respectively. Senators are more likely to quote the Bible or Shakespeare—as Southern Baptist Sam Ervin frequently did during the Senate Watergate hearings—than Hugh Hefner or Kurt Vonnegut in support of an argument.

All one-hundred senators in the 94th Congress listed a religious affiliation. Sixty-six belong to six mainline Protestant denominations (Episcopal and Methodist with sixteen and seventeen respectively; Presbyterian, fifteen; Baptist, nine; United Church of Christ, six; Lutheran, three. Another two listed themselves as Protestant. The remainder included: Churches of Christ, two; Roman Catholic, fifteen; Latter-Day Saints (Mormon), four; Unitarian-Universalist, four; Jewish, three; Christian Science, one; Eastern Orthodox, one; Schwenkfelder, one. The latter is a Pennsylvania sect of German Lutheran origin to which Senator Richard S. Schweiker belongs.

The Senate sits in a half circle facing the presiding Vice-President of the United States whose confusing title is "President of the Senate." Democrats sit at his right; Republicans at his left. But this is an artificial division, for votes are frequently split between conservatives and liberals of both parties. Southern Democrats, for example, may join conservative Republicans in favoring higher defense expenditures and in opposing new social programs.

In the crossfire of political battle it often goes unnoticed that many on both sides justify their positions on religious grounds. For instance, Harold Hughes and John McClellan (D.-Ark.), a Southern Baptist, exchanged verbal blows during the 1974 debate over capital punishment. "What other punishment is 'just' for a man, found to be sane, who would stab, strangle, and mutilate eight student nurses?" demanded the outraged McClellan. "The death penalty is needed to protect the innocent," he stormed, adding a verse from the Old Testament to bolster his argument.

Hughes, known for his literal interpretation of the commandment, "Thou shalt not kill," stood in opposition and solemnly quoted from descriptions of hanging ("his eyes pop almost out of his head, his tongue swells"), electrocutions ("The hands turn red, then white, and cords of the neck stand out like steel bands"), and gasings ("Their eyes pop, they turn purple, they drool"). "In God's name," he begged his colleagues, "join me in rejecting death, affirming life, rejecting vengeance, and affirming redemption."

This is only one of many issues on which the senators who pray together disagree. Generally, conservatives such as McClellan, Stennis, and Curtis will be found voting together, while opposed by moderates like Hatfield. On some issues and in life style however, they may be very close: believing in the same evangelical doctrine, advocating traditional family morality, and adhering to a strict policy of honesty. Stennis, for example, a trustee at Washington's National Presbyterian Church, bears an untarnished reputation for personal integrity in Washington. Reflecting the views of his white Bible Belt constituency, Stennis is a militant foe of pornography, illicit drugs, and forced racial integration of schools. Because of his record on civil rights at least one black Washington taxi driver says, "I will not let him into my cab." But in Mississippi he is hailed as a "great Christian statesman" by white voters who keep sending him back to Washington.

The seat next to Stennis in the Senate chamber belongs to Herman Talmadge, a Southern Baptist layman who frequently fills pulpits in his home state of Georgia. Next to Talmadge is West Virginia's Jennings Randolph, a tall thick-shouldered man who is past 70 but looks 15 years younger. Randolph, the only Seventh Day Baptist in Congress, is a former vice-chairman of the North American Baptist Fellowship of the Baptist World Alliance.

Randolph's homespun, corn-pone drawl is deceptive. No hick, he graduated magna cum laude from Salem College in Salem, West Virginia, taught journalism, served as a college dean, edited a newspaper and magazine and became an accomplished flier and aviation executive before being elected to the House in 1932. After his election to the Senate in 1958, he perhaps did more than any other man to advance the once backward economy of his mountain state.

Admirers call him the "humanitarian Senator." They point to his influence in such legislative efforts as lowering the voting age to 18, providing special aid to the handicapped (an operation years ago saved him from blindness), spearheading environmental and pollution control bills, and establishing new standards in mine safety. Detractors believe that as chairman of the influential Public Works Committee he has been too friendly to the road building industry. He authored the legislation that led to the establishment of the National Interstate Highway system.

Randolph has been deeply involved with church-state issues. He engineered legislation that absolves people from "working on their day of religious observance," a benefit to Jews, Seventh-Day Adventists, and his own small Seventh-Day Baptist denomination. Contrary to those fearing violation of the constitutional mandate of church-state separation, he believes that prayers should be permitted in public buildings and that churches should be permitted to sponsor public housing projects. As an example of the latter, he points proudly to a federally funded low-income housing project in Salem jointly sponsored by a black church and the Junior League, composed of young women from well-to-do Charleston families.

Randolph worries about the increase of divorce, marital unfaithfulness, and undisciplined children. "The strength of our country is the family," he says, and he believes prayer can strengthen the family. "I pray daily with my wife just as my father and grandfather prayed with their families before us."

The West Virginian is concerned about "efforts to legalize and make marijuana look good." He keeps up a running correspondence with the Motion Picture Association over the "deterioration of movies." He feels that the media give the fullest coverage to bad news while playing down good news. "An editor once told me that nice stories are not news. I told him people would react favorably if they are exposed enough to wholesome stories."

Nebraska's Carl Curtis shares Randolph's concern over media preoccupation with bad news. "This dissatisfaction among the population, this mistrust of Congress is caused by emphasis among the news media on evil to the point that readers do not get an objective story. People just do not think that politicians in general are honest. Oh, they believe in *their* Congressman or Senator, but not the rest, just as they'll criticize the medical profession while insisting that their family doctor is different.

"Look at it another way. I had an uncle who preached for over sixty years. One of his hobbies was to keep track of all the people he married—to check on them, encourage them, find out how they were getting along, and tell them he was praying for them. I visited him before he died and asked if any of the couples he had married had been divorced. He said, 'Not to my knowledge.' The first time he made a state newspaper was when his obituary was printed. If he had repudiated his faith with some wild sermon or engaged in misconduct, he would have been known to everyone in Nebraska."

A rock-hard political conservative, Curtis thinks government spends too much money and has become too powerful. His political philosophy is close to that of Barry Goldwater, for whom he served as floor manager at the 1964 Republican National Convention.

The Nebraskan was one of the staunchest opponents of impeachment of Richard Nixon until the former president under court order released tapes disclosing his cover-up role in Watergate. After Nixon resigned in the ensuing furor, Curtis was asked if compassion for the former president should take precedence over the legal process. "This is a time not [only] for compassion," he replied, "but for fairness and reasonableness. For civil authorities to proceed further is not a matter of compassion but of justice."

A mild-mannered, soft-spoken man not given to showmanship, Curtis was elected to Congress in 1938 and to the Senate in 1954. Friend and foe alike say one of the main reasons he has been reelected term after term is his unquestioned integrity. "Honesty is a politician's greatest asset," he believes. "People who disagree with him on all but the most crucial issues will support him if they believe in his integrity. But a politician has to watch out about becoming a Pharisee. I could make a fervent [religious] speech, send it out, and fool a thousand people. But it would be wrong. And as a Christian it would be most insincere of me to use the Gospel to get votes."

Curtis is also active in Washington's National Presbyterian

Church. Curtis thinks the nation's basic problem is "theological, not political. It is lack of basic acceptance of simple Christian doctrine which is absent from many pulpits. Why, lots of people [can't even] recite the Ten Commandments.

"Too many church leaders are saying there are no absolutes. They say Christ was just a fellow with a lot of good ideas. They disregard the authority of God which He has vested in parents and government. We've got to get back to the source of authority. We've accepted relativity in everything and there is no answer in too many instances."

Like Randolph, Curtis believes the concept of separation of church and state has been "carried to ridiculous ends. The founding fathers simply didn't want a state religion such as England had. School [authorities] today think they can't have a minister to give the invocation at graduation exercises. Occasionally I read a denominational magazine that says the elimination of public prayer [in the schools] was a good thing. What's wrong with public recognition that God exists?"

In a statement he entitled, "Why I Believe," Curtis asserts his personal credo:

God has not kept man guessing as to His existence. God has revealed Himself to man through the Bible and Christ... It is not at all hard for me to accept the belief that Christ is divine, that Christ is God. His earthly life was flawless. His teachings are flawless. Whenever His teachings are followed, everything goes all right. Whenever His teachings are ignored, things go wrong. Christ [died] for the salvation of man. [He died] so that he might be resurrected and thus reveal to man the infinite plan and purpose of God ... I have experienced Him. He has guided me and helped me beyond my expectations and far beyond what I deserve. He has consoled me and strengthened me. In time of trial, He has saved me from trouble. He has answered my prayers even though I do not understand why He has sometimes answered 'No.'

I believe, however, He knows best... I have come to
believe in Christ and accept Him in response to all
the instruction I have received since my childhood.
And my faith, based on the witness within me,
grows greater every day.

George McGovern shares many of Carl Curtis's evangelical
roots, although he is far more theologically liberal than his
elder colleague. And politically, he is poles apart from the
Nebraska conservative on the involvement of government in
social-economic issues.

After his disastrous defeat for the presidency in 1972, the
twangy, Bible-quoting South Dakotan all but dropped from
the public eye. But he is still a voice in the Senate, advocating
the application of moral principles, as he sees them, to
national issues.

The presidential campaign smoke over McGovern's
seemingly farfetched proposals to make America a "moral"
nation obscured the man. He is not the wild-eyed political and
religious radical that some conservative evangelicals have
supposed him to be.

McGovern, who holds a Ph.D from Northwestern
University, does not talk as much about his religious faith as
he once did. He did not include in his 1974 *Congressional
Directory* biography the fact that he once pastored a Methodist
church in Illinois. One of the best and most comprehensive
self-descriptions of his Christian faith as it relates to political
life was given in an October 1972 speech at Wheaton College
in suburban Chicago, the alma mater of Billy Graham and
many other evangelical leaders. McGovern recalled his
fundamentalist upbringing as the son of a Wesleyan minister.

"In our family, there was no drinking, smoking, dancing,
or card playing. So you can see why I feel so much at home
here at Wheaton." That brought down the house. Then he
quickly added that "daily teaching from the Scripture, and a
constant immersion in faith, made an indelible imprint on
me."

He admitted to "a period of mild rebellion against some of
the rigidity of my early years," but after service in World War

II as a bomber pilot, a "pattern started to unfold in my life. I felt called into the work of serving others. At first, I thought my vocation was in the ministry, and I enrolled in seminary [Garrett, a liberal Methodist school in Illinois]. During that year, I served as a student pastor and grew in many ways. I thought about my vocation, for I knew, as my mother told me, that a man should not go into the ministry unless he was certain God was calling him there. After a period of deep reflection, I decided I should become a teacher. Yet, even in my teaching ... I still felt there was something else for me to do—and that is what finally led me into politics."

Several points in his speech seemed straight out of the typical conservative evangelical's unstated political philosophy.

—"The Bible teaches that government is to serve man, not that men are the servants of government... Power is ordained by God for the purpose of doing good for the people.

—"All that we seek in our society will not come solely from government. The greatest challenges of our age defy purely political answers... Our deepest problems are within us—not as an entire people—but as individual persons.

—"We must have a fundamental stirring of our moral and spiritual values if we are to reclaim our true destiny.

—"The political process tends to reflect and channel spiritual trends. There are encouraging signs in our land that we are undergoing a new awakening. The sophisticated 'God is Dead' talk now seems as irrelevant as a passing fad—which is what it was. Instead the 'Jesus Movement' and other manifestations of spiritual hunger summon millions back to belief."

He parted company, however, with the philosophy that relegates important issues of humanity to political status and then says Christians should stay out of politics. "Some Christians believe we are condemned to live with man's inhumanity to man—with poverty, war, and injustice—and that we cannot end these evils because they are inevitable. But I have not found that view in the Bible. Changed men can change society, and the words of Scripture clearly assign to us the ministry and the mission of change."

Four weeks later McGovern's hopes were buried under the Nixon landslide. He went back to the Senate a lonely, deeply disappointed (and some say "bitter") man. In 1974 he won reelection by fewer than 16,000 votes.

The personable, handsome Mark Hatfield, who was voted the best dressed man in government in 1974 by the Fashion Foundation of America, is perhaps the best known evangelical senator. He is more difficult to peg in the political spectrum than either McGovern or Curtis.

Hatfield is closer to Harold Hughes in faith and doctrine than to George McGovern yet was the most outspoken Senate dove on the Viet Nam War. He voted with conservatives on the abortion issue, but his continued opposition to American involvement in Southeast Asia brought condemnation from many of his conservative evangelical brethren. He received numerous letters—some addressed "Dear *Former* Brother in Christ"—blasting him for speaking against Nixon's Viet Nam policies, and charging that by opposing God's representative—the President—he was going against God and Scripture. "I've never sought political popularity," he counters, "just political respect."

His warnings about the danger of conservative Protestants "failing to distinguish between the god of an American civil religion and the God who reveals Himself in the Holy Scriptures" have not been appreciated by many of his evangelical brethren. "If we as leaders appeal to the god of civil religion," he told the 1973 National Prayer Breakfast, "our faith is in a small and exclusive deity, a loyal spiritual advisor to power and prestige, a defender of the American nation, the object of a national folk religion devoid of moral content. But if we pray to the biblical God of justice and righteousness, we fall under God's judgment for calling upon His name, but failing to obey His commands."

A few weeks later, after Watergate became a national scandal, Hatfield spoke at Mayor Richard Daley's Prayer Breakfast in Chicago and asked, "Why do we want so desperately to believe in man-centered power? Why do we want to place such a total and uncritical faith in our institutions? Why is it that each of us wants to believe that God blesses America more than He blesses any other land? I believe it is because we have let the wellsprings of deep spiritual faith in our lives run dry."

By this time Hatfield had lost his welcome at the White House, even though he had nominated Richard Nixon for the presidency at the 1960 Republican Convention and supported many Nixon policies.

The disclosure of presidential profanity and deleted expletives in White House tape transcripts of Watergate conversations fired Hatfield's belief that Americans, particularly conservative evangelicals, tend to accept a public relations image of their president. "Presidents Truman, Kennedy, and Johnson all used very earthy language," he alleges. "But here we have a man who tended to let his P.R. men project him as a refined, distinguished, religious person. Now people find the image totally shattered by what he did in private."

Hatfield feels that his old friend Billy Graham helped enhance this image by association with the former president. "I've had people tell me that Mr. Nixon is obviously a Christian because he had Billy Graham preach in the White House or because his mother was a dear Christian woman. They wouldn't say that about the person sitting next to them in the pew in the evangelistic meeting. They'd want a confession from that individual that he is a Christian. Yet they wouldn't demand that from a person occupying a high position if he has the symbols of religious faith.

"The transcripts expose the humanity of high exalted office. They show the blemishes and deficiencies of humanity, the sinfulness of man, the hellishness of exalting and almost idolizing the presidency. In spite of all the Hail-to-the-Chief pomp and circumstance, we found they [the President and his aides] were frail human beings. This can be a very good therapy for all of us."

Hatfield now worries that fear and insecurity will cause people to "look to an authoritarian figure who can give simplistic answers or guarantees of salvation. History has demonstrated that in periods of trouble man tends to turn to this kind of leader for security."

He feels that a leader "who can make a difference" should have five distinctly Christian qualities:

1. Purpose: "He is committed, not to a cause or an ideal, but to a person. He knows whom he serves, and he knows also that he cannot serve two masters. He does not feel the frustration of being compelled to please everyone."

2. Power: "Power and authority do not frighten him, though he respects them; he knows his life is bound up in the One who has ultimate authority and ultimate power."

3. Perspective: "His education, environment and physical well-being all take their proper place in his life: none is put out of proportion... Material things are seen as means to serve God through their proper use, rather than ends in themselves."

4. Peace: "He sees every man, without prejudice or favoritism, as a creation of God, redeemed or potentially redeemed by Christ. Thus, even though he may disagree with another person's ideas, he can accept and respect the other person on the basis of their shared origin... [He] can become a true peacemaker among other men, for he will radiate the attitude of peace in all his relationships."

5. A servant: "He serves for the sake of service, not for the rewards ... He cannot isolate himself from the needs of the world, and when he encounters those needs, he is compelled to try to fill them ... He knows he should be no less concerned for man's total well-being than was Christ, who instructed that 'whoever would be great among you must be your servants.' "[1]

The faith which undergirds Hatfield's political commitment is, in his own words, "a simple faith in a personal transcendental experience with Jesus Christ.... It is both an inward journey to find the true purpose of my own life and an outward journey to be of service to others."[2]

Like McGovern, Hatfield was raised in a devout home (Baptist), fought in World War II, taught political science (Willamette University near the Oregon capitol), and decided to put his ideas into practice by entering politics. Three years later, at age 31, when he was doubling as an Oregon legislator and as dean of Willamette, he made a life-changing commitment to Christ.

"That night in the quiet of my room the choice was suddenly made clear. I could not continue to drift along as I had been doing, going to church because I had always gone, because everyone else went, because there wasn't any particular reason not to go. Either Christ was God and Savior and Lord or he wasn't; and if he were, then he had to have all my time, all my devotion, all my life."[3]

The next evening Hatfield asked Doug Coe, the Navigator staffer who later joined ICL, to accompany him on a speaking engagement. While driving along he told Coe of his commitment and agreed to meet regularly with Coe for Bible study. Subsequently, as faculty sponsor for the Willamette Inter-Varsity Christian Fellowship chapter, Hatfield met several key evangelical leaders, including Bill Bright of Campus Crusade for Christ, Carl Henry of *Christianity Today*, and Richard Halverson. He has been closely identified with them ever since.

His students helped him launch his first campaign. As he walked across the campus to the state capitol to file as a candidate for Marion County representative, they marched behind in a band, playing "The Battle Hymn of the Republic." Through his more than two decades in politics students have remained his most faithful supporters. For example, at the height of massive student dissent over the American and South Vietnamese invasion of Cambodia in 1970, when he was under fire from many evangelical leaders for opposing government policy, Hatfield spoke at Fuller Seminary, an evangelical school in Pasadena, California. As he stood to speak, students in the balcony unfurled a banner reading, "We're with you, Mark."

His rise from the Oregon legislature to the U. S. Senate was meteoric. At thirty-six he was the nation's second-youngest governor. Two years later, in 1960, he nominated Nixon for the presidency, gave the keynote speech at the 1964 Republican National Convention, and won a Senate seat in 1966. In 1972 he won reelection by a 68,000 vote majority over Democratic maverick Wayne Morse. After the election he learned that McGovern had considered him as a running mate.

He believes it is now "imperative" to decentralize political and economic power, giving local neighborhoods and communities "genuine political, economic, and ecological self-determination." This, he thinks, includes saving the republic "from the growing dominance of 'presidential government,'" as well as reducing "excessive concentration of power" in other government institutions, big corporations, and labor unions. He has proposed a reduction of one million civilians and 380,000 military personnel in the federal work force, legislation to insure union democracy, and tax reform. He feels neighborhood government could become the "most dynamic force within our society today."

But he does not think the nation can be renewed without change in individual character. He sees a "crisis of values and human relationships," a "vanishing of love and care," which can only be met in "the spiritual dimension of life." In his own life this involves "a personal, daily relationship with Jesus Christ ... which gives me a base—an absolute—both for my personal and my public life."[4]

Although a member of the Conservative Baptist denomination, Hatfield attends Halverson's Fourth Presbyterian Church with his wife Antoinette (he met her when she was a college counselor) and four children. Here he picked up a copy of Abraham Lincoln's 1863 proclamation for "A Day of Humiliation, Fasting, and Prayer" which had been reprinted on new parchment by Washington interior decorator Ray Bates. Hatfield deleted Civil War references, updated the document to fit present times, then introduced it as a resolution in the Senate for national observance on April 30, 1974. It passed the Senate unanimously but died in a House committee. However, Dr. Thomas A. Carruth, a professor at Asbury Theological Seminary, and other supporters rented a wide-area telephone line to promote the Hatfield idea. Thirty governors proclaimed the Day in their states, but observance nationwide was spotty. The most dramatic demonstration was a vigil before the White House by a group (led by a Baptist street preacher) who marched back and forth for twenty-four hours in sackcloth and ashes. Hatfield spoke at National Presbyterian Church that day calling for a national repentance that "saves us from self-righteousness—from pride that manifests itself in extreme nationalism." He implored the nation to pull away from a "Brand X mentality" that indulges its citizens in affluence and convenience while two-thirds of the deaths annually throughout the world are caused by starvation or related diseases.

Ironically, Hatfield was criticized by the Baptist Joint Committee for Public Affairs for promoting civil religion because he had introduced the resolution into the Senate. He countered that Lincoln's civil religion was "different from that which we see and which I criticize today. He never presumed to imply that God was on his side of an issue. Never once did he employ God to give victory to the North. He was calling for confession, for God's wisdom. He wasn't trying to sanctify a nation, society, party, system of government, or economics."

Hatfield speaks from strong religious conviction, as do others of his Senate prayer group brothers who disagree with some of his views. But they are with him when he says:

> If the Christian faith is to have any effect on the mechanics of government, it must be through the lives of public officials coming together in God... The prayer breakfast groups in the Senate and House of Representatives create a kind of fellowship in which we can humble ourselves together before God.... They meet out of a recognition that they need God's guidance and grace in carrying out their public duties.[5]

CHAPTER SEVEN

Christians
in the House

Conservative columnist James Kilpatrick observed in
mid-1974 that many of the 435 members of the U.S. House of
Representatives* are "models of integrity," while "there are
others who make up the biggest bunch of nickel grafters in
town."[1] He may be exaggerating, but it is a fact that a 1974
Harris Poll showed only 20 per cent of the American people
believed their congressmen were doing a good job.

Many congressmen are acutely aware of the public
diagnosis of their moral health. "In fourteen years in
Washington I've never seen so much mail reflecting such
disgust, disenchantment, and disbelief," said Republican
John Anderson from Rockford, Illinois, in an interview.
"Almost anything one does is subject to challenge on the
grounds that maybe he is doing it for some ulterior motive, or
seeking to evade the law. The general suspicion is really
depressing."

Anderson's colleagues tend to share his dismay. But they
also point out that the House is more representative of the
people than any other governmental body. "The voters get in
Congress what they deserve," is a frequently repeated
comment.

That Congress is indeed a reflection of society can be seen

*Actually 439 sit in the House. Four represent territories outside the 50 states (The
District of Columbia, Puerto Rico, Guam, and the Virgin Islands). They may participate
but cannot vote.

117

in the variety of elected representatives serving in the House. Deep-South whites sit on committees with black activists. Aging male chauvinists deal with dominant females like Bella Abzug. Ivy league philosophers swap opinions with good ole country boys who may think Rousseau was an old time catcher for the Baltimore Orioles.

A wide variety of occupations are represented in the historic chamber that, like the Senate, is replete with religious symbols. Besides lawyers, who lead the list, there are teachers, farmers, businessmen, engineers, preachers, doctors, housewives, pilots, policemen, a veterinarian, and even a professional football quarterback.

In religious affiliation they tend to be more representative of the population than the Senate. With Roman Catholics leading in the 94th Congress (108), followed in order by Methodists (68), Presbyterians and Episcopalians (50 each), Baptists (48), there were also members of 21 additional religious groups. Six House members listed no affiliations. Interestingly, Democratic gains in the 1974 Congressional elections show up in church representations. Democratic and Catholic political fortunes tend to flow together, thus the Democratic landslide of '74 elected the largest number of Catholics to Congress in American history. Correspondingly, Presbyterian politicians are more inclined to be Republican. The '74 Republican debacle reduced Presbyterian ranks in the House from 66 to 50. Altogether, a far *greater* percentage are church members than the average of Americans as a whole. The listings, however, are partly deceiving, for relatively few House members are active in Washington area churches when Congress is in session, and many seldom attend on weekends when they are back home.

About 10 percent participate voluntarily in the House Thursday prayer breakfast. These representatives are more likely to be devoted to their respective churches and concerned about relating their faith to political life.

The prematurely white-haired John Anderson is a prayer group regular and one of the most respected House members. A graduate of Harvard Law School, he is father of five and an active member of the Evangelical Free Church, a small evangelical body with Scandinavian roots. He has authored two books *(Between Two Worlds* and *Vision and Betrayal in America)* and edited another *(Congress and Conscience)* on Christianity and politics. Now chairman of the House Republican Conference, it is said that he could have succeeded Gerald Ford in the important post of Minority Leader of the House if party leaders could have trusted him to vote their way all the time. Instead, say observers, Anderson has a reputation of voting his conscience on sensitive issues. ("If I had that kind of record as a congressman," commented a *Time* reporter privately, "I'd want it engraved on my tombstone.")

"I've been ridiculed by some Republican colleagues for acting on my feelings of moral conscience rather than for political advantage," Anderson acknowledges. "They think I'm pointing my finger at them and saying they have less conscience. I don't want to be self-righteous, but on the other hand I don't want to become so lacking in resolve that I succumb to that kind of pressure. I think the most important thing I can do is show that I'm willing to follow the dictates of a Christian conscience, even at the expense of losing office." Anderson was one of the successful Republican survivors in '74.

Anderson has put his political future on the line more than once by voting against the wishes of many constituents. For example, he cast the deciding vote in the Rules Committee for an open housing bill on the eve of Dr. Martin Luther King's funeral. Two years earlier he had voted against open housing. He says his decision to switch came through prayer and meditation on a Bible passage: "For if a man is in Christ he becomes a new person altogether ... All this is God's doing, for he has reconciled us to himself through Jesus Christ; and he has made us agents of the reconciliation."[2]

While acting on conscience may have alienated some voters in his conservative seven-county district, and even some fellow evangelicals elsewhere, it has earned him a reputation for integrity. To many of his constituents, he has become the "thinking man's conservative," even if some of his votes have not followed party lines.

Anderson is only one of a growing number of congressmen, both veterans and newcomers, who seem to be seriously applying their faith to public life. Florida's Charles E. Bennett, an elder in the Riverside Christian Church in Jacksonville, Florida, chaired the first House Ethics Committee and has been the principal advocate for ethical reforms in Congress. He has not missed a roll call vote in the House since 1951—a record unequaled in the history of Congress.

Bennett, an Eagle Scout and World War II hero, grew up in a poor but devout Disciples of Christ family in then scandal-ridden Tampa. "Some of the most prominent families were procurers in prostitution and drugs, and helped elect corrupt officials," he recalls. "As a Christian teenager I decided I would one day run for public office and do what was right."

Fired with this ambition, Bennett worked his way through the University of Florida (he was president of the student body) and law school, became an attorney, and began his political career as an elected member of the Florida House of Representatives. After he completed nearly five years of military duty, the voters of his district sent him to Congress.

Besides his contributions to ethics legislation, Bennett has promoted military-justice reform and sponsored key bills relating to environment, conservation (he received the Izaak Walton League's Award for "Outstanding Conservation Accomplishment"), safety, and government economy. (For the latter he received the "Watchdog of the Treasury" award from the National Association of Businessmen.)

Like Anderson, Bennett has not always pleased his colleagues. He has always voted against Congressional pay raises. "We're paid too much," he grumbles. "We lose touch with the common people." (Annual pay in 1974 was $42,500 plus an expense account and other miscellaneous benefits relating to official duties.)

Bennett does not apologize for his crusades in ethics and economy. "A public official must be like Caesar's wife, above reproach," he says. "He has the responsibility not only to be right but to appear right."

Still he believes there are more congressmen with integrity than is commonly supposed. "We're continuously running for office, putting our character on the block every two years for anybody to shoot at. Anything negative is ammunition for the opponent's gun. It would be strange if Congress were not a little more moral, a little more strait-laced than the population in general."

Bennett is concerned about what he views as "slippage in parental discipline today. This is hurting our young people. We parents ought to be firm about what type of conversation is allowed in the home. We should take our children to church and Sunday school."

The church, he believes, is the only institution that can work for strong morality in American society. "Congress can't remake the soul of America," he asserts. "If we could, all we'd have to do is pass a law, appropriate a hundred billion dollars, go home and everybody would be good. But goodness comes out of one's relationship to God and fellow human beings."

Republican John Duncan, a drawling former mayor of Knoxville, Tennessee, is cast in the same mold as Bennett. A Presbyterian elder who regularly fills pulpits around his district, Duncan reminisces about his country parents: "Rain or shine, they took ten children to church. My dad taught Sunday school and mother collected used clothes for poor people. They taught me to love and understand people and to realize my position may not be the only right one on an issue.

"We lived halfway between the small towns of Huntsville and Helenwood. Folks going by would always stop and rest on our front porch and talk. One of our problems nowadays is we don't take time to talk to one another. I think one of the worst things that ever happened was when they stopped building houses with big front porches."

The folksy Duncan was elected to the House in 1964 where he serves on the influential Ways and Means Committee, which processes all tax legislation. One of the duties he most enjoys is nonofficial—showing visiting high school groups around the Capitol.

"I always take groups to the little prayer room off the

rotunda and talk to them about the spiritual foundations of
our country. I quote George Washington where he said,
'There is no government without morality, no morality
without religion, and no religion without God.' Then I tell
them about the Mayflower Compact. After returning home,
they write back and say that this [glimpse at America's
spiritual heritage] was what most impressed them in
Washington."

South Carolina Republican Ed Young, a '74 loser, comes
from rural roots. After World War II (he flew 195 combat
missions) he returned home to help his father on the farm
near Florence. He was still farming when he ran for Congress
in 1972 at age fifty-two. He found Congress "exciting and
interesting, but with a certain amount of cynicism. Your ego
becomes overdeveloped because you have so many people
coming to you. I have to get back to the land to reorient my
thinking. I don't want to stay here so long that I develop
'Potomac Fever.' "

Why did he run at fifty-two? "I felt I could do something
for the people in my district! We've had an out migration for
years, people leaving the land and pouring into big city
ghettos. With more industry they could come back to fresh air
and a better life. I have a full time staff member looking into
industry."

Young, a Baptist deacon, went home every weekend while
in Congress to help his wife teach a young adult class in
Sunday school and join three other church members in a live
weekly radio panel program called "The Sunday School
Lesson" on WJMX in Florence.

When in Washington Young said he relied on "the power
of the Holy Spirit. When I'm overcome by all the turmoil and
activity here, I tell myself, 'Now wait a minute. You're trying
to do this all by yourself. You need a greater power.' I say,
'Lord, I don't know the answers. I need your help.' "

Typical of this background, Young is a conservative.
"When I look at the awesome power Congress has to tax and
control and direct people's lives, I become real cautious about
how I vote," he said.

Yet, as is increasingly true among Christian conservatives

on the Hill, his instinct of rugged individualism took second place to a sense of compassion, a reaching out to help the helpless. For example, there was the vote on the minimum wage bill. "I voted against it in 1973," says Young. "When it came up again, my friends in business were sure I would again vote for them. But a black woman came to me and said she had been working at a garment factory for six years without a raise in pay. Her gas had gone up. Her food bill was higher. I knew she and others like her would get a raise only if the minimum wage were increased. So I voted for it." This decision probably contributed to his failure to come back in 1975.

On the other side of the aisle—and political spectrum—from Young is Democrat Walter Fauntroy, a black who got part of his political education in the streets. He is the delegate from the District of Columbia, one of four clergymen in Congress. The others are John Buchanan, Baptist (R.-Ala.); Andrew Young, United Church of Christ (D.-Ga.); Robert J. Cornell (D.-Wis.); and Robert J. Drinan, a Jesuit priest (D.-Mass.). Presbyterian minister William H. Hudnut (R.-Ind.) lost in the '74 elections. Only Fauntroy continues to pastor a church, New Bethel Baptist in Washington, where he has served since 1958.

A Yale Divinity School graduate, Fauntroy was a key leader in the civil rights movement of the sixties, and a prominent figure in Washington's "Home Rule" struggle. He was elected to his post in 1971. He has taken part in the prayer breakfast movement, but he expresses a hint of disillusionment: "I have difficulty understanding how some of my conservative prayer-breakfast white colleagues can continually vote against programs designed to assist the disadvantaged. They are confused. They see oil depletion allowances to wealthy capitalists as okay, but welfare payments to the elderly, sick, and poor as communistic and socialistic. I respect their views, but I think they are wrong and will vigorously oppose their positions."

He also differs with his conservative brethren on whether or not morality and acceptance can be legislated. "It's an escape to say you work in your church and I'll work in mine, and after awhile black and white folks will love the Lord and not discriminate against each other. It isn't that simple. In civil rights we engaged in the politics of creative tension until we could open up the political process. That was the way we got our voting rights bill, and the beneficiaries are two million blacks registered in the South today."

Civil rights supporters have helped Fauntroy build a strong power base in Congress. "In 1965 there were only 400 black elected officials in the nation," he said in an interview prior to his successful 1974 election campaign. "Today there are over 3,000. We're going to elect 500 more in the South this year. Many of these black officials marched with us in the South [Fauntroy coordinated the Selma to Montgomery march and the "Poor People's Campaign" in 1969]. When we were trying to get Congress to vote home rule for the District of Columbia, I asked each black elected official throughout the nation to write his congressman to support home rule. The result was that thirty-seven congressmen broke with tradition and provided the margin to get the bill through."

When it comes to voting, Fauntroy says he's guided by the New Testament. "I ask God to show me what is best for the 'least of these' [a quote from Jesus]. I assume He is on their side. For example, I put in a homestead act which will let poor people buy defaulted city property for $1 if they can rehabilitate it. And I support penal reform and rehabilitation. The question here is, 'Can the cost to one group be fashioned into an investment for the welfare of all concerned?' It's going to cost tax money to train prisoners for jobs. I think it's worth it."

The other black minister in the House is Andrew Young, the first black man in 100 years to win the Democratic nomination for Congress from a southern district. A quiet, deliberate man with a conservative hair style and the polish of a banker, Young was elected by the "new Atlanta" in 1972. Known as a moderate, he was the only black congressional representative to vote for the confirmation of Gerald Ford as vice-president. In 1974 he was included in *Time's* portfolio of 100 young leaders with the most potential for civic and social impact. Young grew up in a middle class black family in New

Orleans where he attended the integrated Central Congregational Church. But he doesn't recall "really studying the New Testament" until a trip home from Howard University in Washington. "I met this young white man preparing for missionary work in Rhodesia. It bothered me that a white was going to give his life for the people of Africa and nobody had ever suggested I could do it."

Young's interest in missionary work deepened as he dug into the New Testament in a search for what God would have him do in life. Upon graduation from Howard he enrolled at Hartford Seminary in Connecticut and applied to the foreign mission board of his denomination. But by the time the board was ready to send him, he was married and heavily involved in the civil rights movement.

His interest in politics developed from "seeing the frustration of black men" in his first church in Thomasville, Georgia. "They were slowly being destroyed by the lack of opportunity. I went to the white businessmen and the mayor, but got only a minimum response. I started talking about a voter registration drive. One thing led to another until Dr. King invited me to join his staff. Two years after his death I ran for Congress and lost. I ran again in 1972 and won."

Young preaches in a church "practically every Sunday" and views himself as "pretty orthodox in theology." He insists that the New Testament "is really explosive when people read it, and take it seriously, and think of themselves as heirs of Christ, partners with God, fellow workmen in the kingdom."

With a grin, he says he now "tries to be a pastor to Congress on issues and to preach from the floor of the House. The only difference is that I don't take a text."

Young sees changes in America's mood. "Since Dr. King's death, I've sensed that white America wants to repent on race and be through with the past. I sense in the majority of blacks a real desire for the system to work and the American dream to become a reality. I have nothing but hope."

In 1973 and 1974 Young met with John Dellenback, a Republican from Medford, Oregon, for prayer each week. A Presbyterian elder, Phi Beta Kappa Yale graduate, and former law professor, Dellenback is "persuaded that if we open ourselves to God's bidding, then each of us in our slots can help in solving the immense national problems that face America."

In a 1974 interview Dellenback said his faith propelled him to run for Congress in 1966. "When my wife, Mary Jane, and I became active in our church, our faith spurred us into community involvement. Suddenly the congressman from our area decided to run for the Senate. We discussed with our pastor and another friend my becoming a candidate for his old seat. We decided to put out the fleece [test the will of God]. I ran and was elected. Congress is where I'm supposed to live out my Christian faith right now. But you don't just sit back and say, 'God, if you want me in Congress, let me be elected.' I intend to do the best job I can campaigning for reelection. It will be up to God whether I win. If not, there'll be no great panic. God will have something else for me to do."

A political moderate with special interest in higher education, he didn't think of himself "as a congressman who is also a Christian." He explained: "I'm a Christian who has been a teacher and a practicing lawyer and who is now a congressman. There's a fundamental difference in what you are first and second. If I'm a Christian first, I can't make my decisions on the basis of what is politically palatable. I must stand for right as best I see it and explain it to my people, hoping they will understand." Apparently they didn't, for he lost in his '74 effort to gain a fifth term.

Another Presbyterian is Richard F. Vanderveen, a Michigan Democrat who at fifty-one in a major upset won the seat Gerald Ford left behind when Ford became Vice President. Vanderveen, an attorney, is a past president of the Michigan Presbyterian men's organization and a former member of the United Presbyterian national missions board. He says it was "impossible to be an active church participant and not feel increasing moral outrage over what had happened within the national [Nixon] administration. But instead of [just] fuming each morning as I read the newspaper, I ran for office when Mr. Ford became Vice President."

Vanderveen made morality and Watergate the main issue of his campaign, defying polls that a month before the special election showed him losing overwhelmingly. He calculated correctly that even the conservative middle Americans of Grand Rapids had become sufficiently outraged to register at the voting booths their protest against what they saw as moral deterioration in national leadership. He apparently wasn't elected on the basis of his churchmanship, for his opponent, Robert Vander Laan, spoke strongly about his faith and its place in politics and was a member of the Christian Reformed Church, the majority denomination in the district.

Interviewed in Washington before his successful bid in the regular '74 election, Vanderveen expressed displeasure at the alleged trappings of civil religion. He said he saw elements of it in the National Prayer Breakfast, Billy Graham's association with then President Nixon, and the Nixon White House church services. He saw in these a sort of religious stamp of approval on the Nixon administration, something Nixon used for political rather than for spiritual benefit. "The White House services, for example, would have been okay," he explained, "but only without the TV cameras and writers and a selective guest list that made them social events."

On the other hand, he is concerned about the "lack of continuing faith and support of institutional religion. The organized church has gotten off the track with too much emphasis on form, ritual, and attendance as the social thing to do," he admits. "Not enough attention is given to substance. I sometimes think of the church as I do the U. N. The whole structure is pretty fragile, but we have to keep working at it."

Some distance north of where Vanderveen's constituents live is the Michigan district of Elford A. Cederberg. Republican Cederberg, a close friend of Gerald Ford, was elected in 1952. Like John Anderson, he is the son of a Swedish immigrant and a member of the Evangelical Free Church denomination.

A much-medaled World War II veteran, Cederberg once managed a small manufacturing company in Bay City, Michigan, and was mayor of the town at twenty-nine. He has mixed feelings about the future of America. For one thing, he says, the country needs the interest and involvement of its young people in government. He acknowledges that many young people are "turned off to politicians," yet he is encouraged by the interest he senses on the part of young people in his district. "They don't believe every person in public life has ulterior motives and is accepting graft. In my years of public life, I have never had anyone suggest I should do something ethically wrong. They know it wouldn't do any good in the first place."

He worries that affluence and moral permissiveness may lead to such softness and lack of resolve that the nation "can't long survive. But whether we would have the stamina to stand up and handle a real economic foreign crisis remains to be seen," he adds.

Cederberg represents a large, rather thinly populated district of farmers, fruit growers, fishermen, and small businessmen and manufacturers—the self-made types who stand by the Protestant work ethic and the stability of institutions. Trent Lott is from a similar twelve-county district in southern Mississippi. An All-American Jack Armstrong type, he is Southern Baptist, as are many of his constituents on the Mississippi Gulf Coast.

Lott learned the congressional ropes as administrative assistant to the veteran William Colmer, the long-time powerful Democratic chairman of the House Rules Committee. When Colmer retired in 1972, Lott won the seat as a Republican and became the first GOP congressman from Mississippi's Fifth District since the days of Reconstruction. He was then only 31.

The young Mississippian was perhaps the quietest member of the House Judiciary Committee that heard Watergate evidence and debated articles of impeachment against Richard Nixon, and he was one of the last two holdouts against recommending Nixon's impeachment. At the time he said, "I don't condone the Watergate mess, but I am concerned about the presidency as an institution. Look at the record: Kennedy assassinated, Johnson hounded out of office, Nixon up for possible impeachment. Is it the man or the institution? We southerners have a lot of respect for the institutions. We believe in patriotism. The flag to us is not just a piece of cloth."

The affable young southerner grew up in the First Baptist Church of Pascagoula where he sang in the choir and was church attorney. He still prefers attending this church where "everybody knows me and I feel at home" to churches around Washington.

Lott is apple pie positive about the American system, "It worked for me. I ran as a Republican in Mississippi with no money and no organization and here I am. If I don't believe that the American dream will work, who in the world will?"

He isn't disturbed about the slowness of Congress. "Is it bad that we can't react quickly?" he asks. "Quite often when we react in a crisis, we act crudely and improperly. Right now everything is energy. If you aren't for it, you're against getting us out of the energy crisis. A couple of years ago we hung our necks on ecology. Now, after Watergate, the cry is reform. What we really need most is decent people in dynamic leadership."

New York's Jack Kemp, another strong defender of the American system, also believes that leadership is primary. "A quarterback doesn't go into a game and ask, 'Does anybody have a good play?' " asserts Kemp, who called signals for the professional Buffalo Bills before coming to Congress in 1970. "He's the leader and is responsible for his actions. The worst seed being planted in our society today is that the individual is no longer responsible for his own moral and economic decisions."

Kemp was also among *Time's* select group of 200 young leaders for the future. A Republican who is also endorsed by the Conservative Party of New York, Kemp has long been active in the Fellowship of Christian Athletes. But he is as much at home in philosophy as in athletics or the Bible. "Today's flexible, situationist philosophy of morality is nothing but an outgrowth of Hegel's dialectical theory of history," he declares. "The Spaniard Ortega y Gassett said of his age, 'We do not know what is happening to us and that is precisely what is happening to us.' Educators are telling young people there are no standards, that everything is relative to time and place. If every person does what he wants at any given moment, there will ultimately be no respect for law, the system, and the institutions. There won't be enough policemen to protect society from the human animals.

"Whether you're in professional football or politics, you need a moral and ethical standard to guide your life, to remind you that there is more to life than yourself. As a congressman I have to manifest a standard of conduct. I have to live the witness, articulate it, and let my light shine."

Kemp is "concerned but not despondent" about the present drift of government and society. "I'm cautiously optimistic. True Christianity is very much alive in this country. I see some spectacular things going on in my community, in New York State, and here in Washington. We had a luncheon for Christian athletes in connection with the National Prayer Breakfast. My wife, Joanne, is very active in the Christian Women's Clubs and in Fourth Presbyterian Church prayer groups. We find the messages of Dr. Halverson at Fourth Church very refreshing. He can explain how Christianity is the answer to the cynicism and the existentialism that has permeated today's western civilization."

Kemp believes the evangelical movement is already producing leaders with higher ethics. "We have now in Congress some really sharp young men of both parties who are excited about what can be done from a Christian perspective and what can't be done. We know the government isn't the sole answer to our problems. It shouldn't be allowed to grow so large as to remove the responsibility of the people."

Arizona's John Conlan stands with Kemp on this issue. "I don't believe the answer is more laws," he says. "I look at a new law and ask, 'Will it suppress human initiative and responsibility or will it encourage it?' People need moral discipline rather than governmental or controlled discipline."

Conlan, forty-four, is one of the brightest conservatives in the House. The son of Hall-of-Fame baseball umpire Jocko Conlan, he graduated from Harvard Law School and won a Fulbright Scholarship to the University of Cologne, Germany. He served in the army, practiced law, and taught political science. When he came to Washington in 1970 he was elected president of the House Republican freshman class.

He describes himself and several other newcomers as "creative conservatives [who are] ... solution oriented."

He warns that a let-government-do-it attitude is a "cancer that must be cured lest it eat the heart out of us. We don't produce anything in government. All we do is rip off the workers. Right now we're picking up almost 40 percent of their pay."

Conlan recalls "drifting into the socialist pattern" during his last year of undergraduate work at Northwestern University. Then he was "reborn through faith in Jesus Christ." That summer he traveled behind the Iron Curtain to see what socialism was "really like." "I came back with different conceptions about man and the universe. But it took three years of studying the Bible at Park Street Congregational Church in Boston, when I was at Harvard, to put biblical principles into practice."

Conlan sees "two basic philosophies worldwide. One starts with God and makes man the minor premise. The other starts with no god and makes man the major premise. Those who believe the latter have been trying to centralize government while we who believe God is primary have been asleep at the switch. The humanists have come a long way. The patient [America] is at a point where it can recover and go on to greater strengths, or it can succumb. It's a question whether the Christian element will elect more honorable men at all levels."

Minnesota's Albert Quie, a long-time close friend of Gerald Ford, is likewise concerned about the movement toward humanism. "We're getting away from religious orientation in trying to be neutral. There's no way we can be neutral. If we were, there would be no moral development at all."

Quie, a member of the American Lutheran Church, still has a wheat and dairy farm in his home state. He has been in Congress since 1958 and is the ranking Republican member of the Committee on Education and Labor.

He links the change of family life styles to present difficulties. "On the farm we ate together. The kids could see what the father did. Now they see him only on weekends. They may not understand what he does for a living. He has little time for them. Communication breaks down and the family is fragmented. With five teen-agers I know how tough it is. We have to work to find time for daily devotions."

Quie thinks television is also a factor in the deterioration of morality. "At one time if a mayor or church leader stole money, for example, it was a traumatic experience for the people. But it was localized. Now television makes the whole country feel the effect of bad news. The immorality that is critical in government is felt throughout the country."

Quie's five teen-agers are involved in the evangelical Young Life movement. He is one of the most active in the Washington prayer groups. He believes that spiritual renewal must come through people, not institutions which, he says, are "not capable of love."

James C. Wright, Jr., a Democrat from Fort Worth, has been in Congress twenty years. A Presbyterian lay worker, he believes that "what we need more than anything else is a revival of a sense of community and togetherness," fueled by "a loving spirit. If we lack the capacity to understand and serve one another, then we have serious troubles ahead."

Wright is especially concerned about water pollution abatement, "one of the really serious challenges which we face today," he says.

"This is one problem where we can all find some unity. The amount of water in the world has not varied since God created the heavens and the earth. There is no such thing as new water. Science tells us a glass of water contains some of the molecules that fell in the flood of Noah, floated fishing boats on the Sea of Galilee, and washed the blood of Normandy beaches on D day. It's a marvel how water is kept in constant rotation, falling on the earth, carried by surface and subterranean streams to the great ocean reservoirs, purified by the sun's magnet. Then conveyed by wind and cloud back to the parched and thirsty earth. We enter into a divine partnership with nature. We can keep it clean and prolong life or we can fail and bring death. We can never live without it."

The veteran Texas House member feels "very inadequate" about dealing with this and other problems in Congress. "No person can be a sufficient authority on the wide range of legislation. We are expected to exert some intelligent judgment. Ultimately when the roll is called, you make one unequivocal monosyllable—yes or no—and just hope and pray that your judgment was right."

Still he believes "God has a plan for each person, nation, and society. I don't know how to reconcile the omnipotence of God with the free will of man. I just know I must try to cultivate the kind of relationship with the Creator that will let me know and follow his plan."

These Christians in the House of Representatives and others in the Senate represent the best of America. They believe essentially the same evangelical theology. They share a common concern for strengthening of the family and community ties, regirding society with moral absolutes, solving serious national problems such as rising crime and environmental pollution, rekindling public optimism, rebuilding individual initiative, and increasing neighborly concern among their fellow Americans. They differ on how some of these goals may be accomplished and which should have priority. But they are united in believing that the basic problem is spiritual and the best and only enduring solution is a relationship with God through Jesus Christ that results in transformation of character.

CHAPTER EIGHT

Rendering unto Caesar

Mark Twain said an idiot and a congressman were one and the same. Will Rogers said he didn't know before he got to Rome that it had senators. "Now I know why it declined," he quipped. Another humorist cracked, "With Congress, every time they make a joke it's a law. And every time they make a law it's a joke." Even the word "bunk" was brought into the language by a congressman in 1820. Whenever Rep. Felix Walker of Buncombe County in North Carolina made a speech on the House floor for the benefit of his constituency, he would say, "This is for Buncombe." "Buncombe," shortened to "bunk," soon came to mean meaningless, useless talk.

With sagging public confidence in our political institutions, the problems of Congress have become less a joking matter. The response of a high school social studies student to his teacher in West Covina, California, reflects what millions feel. "What difference does it make who you vote for?" he said. "Once they're elected they do what they want."[1]

Harold Hughes said he "knew that people were losing faith in the political structure of the nation" when he ran for the Senate in 1968. "But if all I am is a reflecting poll of people back home," he added, "they ought to send a secretary to the Senate. Our job is integrity, not to respond to the latest political poll."

Burnett Thompson, a former Wesleyan Methodist minister

135

who is administrative assistant to Rep. William Whitehurst (R.-Va.) dips into constituent mail to illustrate his contention that a Congressman cannot be all things to all people. "Here's a man who says,'I've put up with your Watergate and your welfare mess. Now my gas bill has gone out of sight and I've had it.' Corruption didn't bother him, but getting hit in the pocketbook did. Here's a Catholic priest who wrote the congressman, 'A man with your background and knowledge of history should be able to put through legislation that will bring us back to normalcy and sanity.' Bill [Whitehurst] answered him, 'It's impossible to legislate moral sanity.' "

Pity the poor besieged congressman who tries to do all that's expected of him by his almost half a million constituents. Every day is a dizzy whirl of ceaseless mail and visitors. The congressman's door must always be open, he and his staff always accommodating. Tennessee's John Duncan has his staff members sign a pledge each January that they will be kind and helpful to everybody.

There's an old story around Washington about a congressman who was spotted at a party with a small black book in his hand. Asked if he was looking to see where he would go next, he replied, "No, I'm trying to find out where I am now." A typical member is in his office by nine A.M. He spends a couple of hours on mail and staff business; studies legislative proposals; sandwiches in talks with reporters, important home folks, and colleagues; hurries to committee hearings; contacts government agencies in the interest of constituents; gulps down lunch; dashes off at the periodic screams of a buzzer to the House floor for roll-call votes; listens to important debate; and squeezes in visits with the more important callers who "happen to be in Washington and just dropped by to see our congressman." Evenings there are receptions and other social gatherings, and often a briefcase full of work to do at home, not to mention family obligations.

Because of such pressure, says Arizona's John Conlan, "We have very little time to sit back and think through how we got where we are, how we can get out of problems, and how we can increase productivity and moral character among our people."

Take just participation in committees where, according to Rep. Charles Bennett, "the real work of Congress is done."

Every new bill of substance is first referred to a standing committee for discussion and testimony by expert witnesses. Parts of the legislation may be assigned to subcommittees for more detailed work. If the standing committee reports the bill out favorably, it is placed on the congressional calendar for reading and debate within the full House. There it may be amended and sent back to committee. If and when it is finally passed, the bill goes to the Senate where the committee process starts all over again. Should the Senate want changes, it is assigned to a special House Senate Conference committee for compromise. The original House and Senate committees study the result and if they agree it has been drawn correctly, the Speaker of the House and the President of the Senate sign the bill and send it to the White House for the President's signature. Should the chief executive opt to veto, the bill may return for another vote (two-thirds yeas are required to overturn a veto).

The legislation process is so cumbersome and slow that congressmen may not see results of bills they introduce until they are up for reelection—and in some cases defeated and returned to private life. And far more often than not, bills are left to die in committee.

The Legislative Reorganization Act of 1946 cut the standing committees from eighty-one to thirty-seven (twenty-one in the House; sixteen in the Senate). But as government has become larger and more complex, these have spawned 260 subcommittees. The House Education and Labor Committee, for example, has eight subcommittees. And to complicate the process further, a labor or education bill may be referred to still other committees. The number of such referrals in education alone numbers around 1,000 each year.

Once a bill becomes law, it may be administered through a myriad of government agencies. "Duplication is rampant," notes Rep. Albert Quie. "Almost forty different federal agencies administered 294 post-secondary education programs that cost $8 billion in 1972." It thus becomes impossible for the Congress or the Administration to co-ordinate federal policy, Quie contends.

Quie feels the committees must be reduced in number and streamlined. "Some members belong to as many as six or seven subcommittees," he observes. "Often it is impossible for a Member to attend all of his subcommittee meetings on a given day. He has to jump from one to another with the result that he never feels really on top of anything as he would like. Last Congress one of our subcommittees had eighteen members and held seventeen days of hearings. Our three 'best' attenders made fourteen, seven, and five of those hearings."

Quie further proposes that hearings be held around the country. "I do not know a Member who will say he can learn as much in a hearing room as he can visiting with people in a setting where the federal program has direct impact on their lives." A second reason for this decentralization, he says, is to hear from the people who cannot afford to come to Washington and testify before congressional committees. "In education we hear from the Washington-based lobbyists, state officials, city-school superintendents, and a few others. We do not get the benefit of enough school teachers, principals, students, parents, or school board members."

Something approaching an earthquake hit Congress when seventy-five freshman Democrats were swept in over the debris of Watergate during the '74 election. Tending to be liberal and anti-establishment, they joined veteran incumbents who had been chafing for change and successfully overturned the time-honored seniority rule of the House. By taking advantage of a rule that liberals won two years before, requiring a separate vote by House Democrats on each chairmanship at the start of a new Congress, they unseated three powerful Southerners from committee chairmanships. This put committee chairmen—usually more conservative than rank-and-file House Democrats—on notice that they will have to shape up to majority views or risk being dumped. Conservatives have responded cautiously, with some warning that too much change too fast is dangerous.

More structural reform of both parties is likely to come in

time, hopefully permitting the two houses to become more efficient and democratic. But internal changes will not do much to ease the pressures and temptations from outside special interest groups.

The halls of the Capitol and adjacent office buildings are awash with more than ten registered lobbyists for each Senator and House member. They represent industrialists, manufacturers, cotton growers, milk producers, school teachers, brewers, craft unions, doctors, airlines, conservationists, and all other special interests in America strong enough to send their voices to Washington.

The primary job of these lobbyists is to protect their employers from higher taxes and hurtful regulations and practices, and to otherwise advance their self interest. Yet it is the rare congressman who does not acknowledge the value of good lobbyists. They are specialists in an area where most congressmen probably have little, if any, expertise. They can provide background information essential to intelligent legislative analysis—and voting. John Conlan says he listens "if they can make a good presentation." Trent Lott considers lobbying "part of an education process. If you don't have someone from the cotton growers, you don't know their position. But you don't have to take what they say as gospel."

A comparatively new breed on the Washington scene are the so-called "people's lobbyists." Spawned by Ralph Nader and activist groups, they speak for concerned citizens who can't afford to come to Washington. Legislators know that they spell votes and listen. For example, Nader and anti-smoking groups succeeded in getting a law passed that put smokers in the back of intercity buses.

This is not all. Congressmen are pressed by thousands of unregistered lobbyists who claim they are just out to "inform" the legislative branch. Legislative aides from the White House and various government agencies come to dispense information and cast influence favorable to their employers.

The harried congressmen are also the target of religious lobbyists on the payrolls of church denominations, councils of churches, and religious coalitions. Many have offices on a street near the Capitol known as "Church Lobby" Row. The religious lobbyists try to travel a two-way street between the denominations they represent and Congress. The Baptist Joint Committee on Public Affairs, for example, attempts to represent the Baptist viewpoint in religious liberty and church-state deliberations. It also sends back to its Baptist constituencies a continuous flow of information, ideas, and analyses of what Congress and government agencies are doing in these areas. Lobbyists of other denominations (particularly Protestants) have similar concerns.

Albert Quie is one of many legislators who want to hear from church groups on church-state issues.

> Whenever the question of taxation of church property comes up in legislative bodies or revenue agencies, the church as an organization is expected to express its views and deal directly with the state in receiving tax exemption. Similarly, when the government purchases services for hospital, welfare and feeding programs administered by churches, it deals directly with the churches in the preparation and operation of these programs. Finally, because of the effect public-education policy has on parochial education, the organized church is directly concerned with the formulation of that policy. Where aid for higher education is received directly, or where public policy on education influences church-related education, the church not only has the opportunity to speak out, but we should expect it to do so.[2]

If the religious lobbyists stopped with church-and-state matters, they probably would engender little controversy. But representatives of major member denominations of the National Council of Churches, for example, have lobbied Congress on amnesty of draft evaders and deserters, abortion, welfare reform, strip mining, health care, and other issues upon which their constituencies are sorely divided.

Burnett Thompson, administrative aide to Virginia's Whitehurst says, "These guys claim to represent their denominations, but we know that people are divided over issues they lobby us on. I remember one fellow who came into our office. The congressman was tied up and couldn't talk to him so he gave me his pitch. When he said, 'I'm speaking for 11 million Methodists,' I told him, 'Wait a minute. I'm a Methodist, and you don't speak for me.' "

Conservative congressmen, especially, do not seem to appreciate religious lobbyists who press them on controversial matters. "I don't see them very much," says Charles Bennett. "When I do I'm not impressed because they aren't talking about the things of Christ. They're usually pushing some political idea that passed at their denominational convention and has nothing to do with the spiritual life of the people. That turns me off."

Jack Buttram, a sandy-haired, soft-spoken South Carolinian, introduces himself as a "Christian lobbyist" when he speaks to church groups. A former faculty member at Bob Jones University, he has held a variety of politically related jobs: press secretary for Senators Strom Thurmond and Paul Fannin, White House Staff aide, public relations representative, and a lobbyist. From his own experience he cites an example of the lobbying problems:

"Most legislators are unaware of the details in a particular situation, such as whether banks can get involved with the businesses to which they loan money. Let's assume you run a dry cleaning business, and you go to the bank for a loan. The bank has an insurance business on the side. So the loan officer says, 'I'm sure you want insurance to cover the loan.' If you want the loan you agree. But the insurance agent across the street would have difficulty selling you the same kind of insurance. That's repeated in auto leasing, travel agencies, security dealerships, and many other businesses. Congress said back in the thirties that banks ought to deal at arm's length with businesses they loan money. But recent rulings of the Federal Reserve Board have changed matters. Now a coalition of businesses have retained me to help get legislation passed so they can operate without unfair competition."

He insists that lobbyists are "no worse than people in any other legitimate profession." But he concedes that Washington has "the kind of power that attracts corruption"

through lobbying by special interest groups. It is no secret
that certain special interest groups channel sizable sums of
money into election campaign coffers. Which side gets the
funds often depends on the record of past favors and
votes—or the prospects of future ones. Usually it is all quite
legal, but the ethics of it is another matter.

Lobbyist Buttram compares political power to sulfuric acid.
"If you keep it in the right container, fine. But if you put it in
a tin can it destroys the can. Put power in the hands of the
wrong people and it becomes destructive. A senator or
representative can be a good container or a weak one. The
weaker they are the sooner they are corrupted. I think the
quality of a man depends primarily on his relationship with
the Creator of the universe."

Florida's Rep. Bennett believes that more is needed "than
the Ten Commandments and the Sermon on the Mount to
deter men from unethical behavior." Bennett himself will not
accept any personal gifts except from his immediate family.
He sends gifts of perishable food to a military hospital, after
notifying the donor of his rule. Other gifts of value are sent
back to the giver. Tennessee's John Duncan has "returned at
times as much as $1,000," and knows of other Congressmen
who have returned money where they knew the giver might
expect something. "You don't read this in the newspaper," he
complains. "You just hear about the bad ones."

Another payoff for favoritism by a government official,
says Bennett, is a well-paying outside job. Bennett helped
prepare the Federal Conflict of Interests Law. This legislation
makes it harder for present or former Federal employees to
receive private benefit from their government work. Upon
discovering that over 2,000 former military officers were
employed by the 100 largest corporations in America, he
introduced a stronger conflict-of-interest bill.

Watergate brought widespread clamor for changes long
demanded by legislators like Bennett. Stories of six-figure
slush funds and bags of $100 bills channeled mysteriously
through Mexican banks roused public indignation. Big Labor
funneled more than $100 million in cash contributions and
other services to candidates (mostly Democrats) in the 1972

and 1974 political campaigns. Big Business also donated huge sums, mostly into Republican campaign chests. Altogether, the 1972 elections are estimated to have cost nearly a half billion dollars, much of which came from special-interest groups.

Some reforms in campaign financing have already been enacted as a result of disclosures relating to Watergate. But Rep. John Anderson of Illinois warns that the special interest groups have "far more tools in their influence kits" than mere campaign cash. "Most important, they have the ability for effective political mobilization."[3]

Anderson says the major lobbies in Washington can mobilize their membership on an hour's notice when an issue urgent to them is at stake. He notes that the National Association of Manufacturers has its entire national membership cross-coded and computerized. When a few votes are needed on crucial legislation, members are urged to bombard target congressmen with telephone calls, telegrams, and even visits from important constituents. Labor unions can provide a similar mass response when their interests are at stake.

Even noneconomic groups can act swiftly with powerful force. As an example, Anderson notes that no legislation affecting veterans ever moves from a committee without the stamp of approval from the Veterans of Foreign Wars.

In a United Press survey Rep. Gerry E. Studds (D.-Mass.) agreed with Anderson that Congress in "nowhere near as representative as it was intended to be. It is extraordinarily spineless... The list of what we haven't done is breathtaking. We've failed to deal, almost without exception, with the major issues of the country." But in the same survey, Barbara Jordan (D.-Tex.), a daughter of a Baptist minister, countered that "if people could see us struggling with the issues behind the scenes, they'd have a greater appreciation."[4]

Rep. James Wright of Texas believes "two snares lie on either side of the path we have to tread. One is cynicism where you begin saying that it's all just a gaudy, worldly game and I might as well join in. The other is self-righteousness, where you can come to feel that you alone have an exclusive franchise to God's will. I still think you can avoid both and make politics a noble affair. The very challenge of walking that tight line can build individual character and serve one's fellow man."

Lamar Baker, a conservative Republican from Tennessee who lost in '74 to his state's first successful woman candidate for Congress, and an elder in the Church of Christ, declared that he never thought he could change the world while in Congress. "You have to work with others," he says. "You can't accomplish anything by yourself unless you've served a long, long time [Baker had two terms] and attained a position of leadership. I can't engage in a ruthless course of domination. I can only associate myself with causes that have value for good. I don't have to decide whether or not I am going to be honest. I made that commitment long ago. But there are little borderline areas where one must follow his judgment."

Jack Kemp, the former professional football player, agrees that choices aren't always simple. "Every issue I'm involved with has right and wrong, truth and fiction. It is a continuing struggle to do what is right. There is nothing in the Bible or the life of Jesus that says it is going to be easy. The choices are difficult. But the struggle becomes dynamic. You continue to be refreshed as you seek guidance under God."

Says John Anderson: "We must be willing to look into the face of political defeat and do what is right and moral even if it is not universally accepted [or expedient]. And we must do this without mock heroics or grandstanding. If there ever was a period in history in the last 100 years when government officials should take a sacrificial attitude towards their careers, that time is now. It is too dangerous to gauge our decisions on the prospect of election in November."

Anderson sounds a prophetic call: "Each and every individual in any and all periods of human history is directly responsible to the Creator, God. And we are called upon by this God not only to acknowledge His being, but to serve Him by serving His justice and His righteousness. He calls us not only to respect justice, and not only to abstain from evil, but to actively pursue justice."

God helping them, he and other Christian legislators propose to do this within Congress.

CHAPTER NINE

Salt in the System

Federal workers seldom make news except when involved in a scandal. They are more often the butt of jokes and bitter sarcasm for inefficiency, waste, and gobbledy-gook. One canard asks, "How many government employees does it take to screw in a light bulb?" Answer: "One to hold the bulb and two to turn the ladder."

Yet these are the people who make government work. Staffers in the legislative, executive, and judicial branches are the hidden brain reserve of their highly visible bosses, churning out press releases and speeches; polling constituents; researching cases, programs and legislation; and handling a plethora of other below-the-surface duties for which they seldom get public credit. Federal agency and commission employees put legs to legislation voted by Congress and/or authorized by the White House. They carry out the programs, make investigations, mail checks, compile reports, and together with congressional and other federal staffers generate billions of pieces of paper each year.

Unfortunately public opinion usually lumps the workers all together, seeing a misshapen lump of bureaucracy growing at an alarming rate, strangling private initiative, and siphoning off consumer purchasing power through increased taxes and other levies. This is unfortunate and unfair, for as in any mass of American workers there are innovators and idealists trying to make the system work for the good of everyone, as well as drones and dullards who furnish more drag than push. Evangelical believers are more evident among the former than the latter. They are active, positive ingredients in the seasoning salt that helps keep government responsive to the needs of the citizenry.

Methodist minister Burnett Thompson is one of some 10,000 who work for members of the House and Senate. (This is more than the entire population of the District when Congress first met in the new Capitol building in 1800.) As Rep. William Whitehurst's administrative assistant, Thompson supervises a press aide, an appointments secretary, and six other staffers—all paid from the Congressman's office allowance.

A bustling, bespectacled, on-the-go man with thinning sandy hair, Thompson graduated from Houghton College, an evangelical school operated by the Wesleyan (Methodist) Church of America. After organizing five Wesleyan Methodist churches in ten years, he enrolled for graduate study at Old Dominion University in Norfolk, Virginia, where he met Whitehurst, then the school's dean of students and a member of the United Methodist Church.

They struck up a friendship. When Whitehurst acknowledged over lunch one day that he knew very little about the Bible, Thompson offered to teach him. Gradually other men joined them and as they began praying about and discussing their roles as Christians in society, they reached the consensus that Whitehurst should run for Congress. "He got 54 percent of the vote the first campaign, 62 percent the second, and 72 percent the third," says Thompson.

Thompson and Whitehurst have one of the closest working relationships on Capitol Hill "because we are Christians." The former pastor says, "If I'm doing my work right, Bill should never have to get involved in anything but committee work, floor work, meeting people, and a few other things. I should be able to help constituents, handle correspondence, and take care of routine press interviews. Because I can usually predict which way Bill is going on an issue, I can give a quote to a newspaper man, then call him up and say 'this is what you told him.' One thing I can't do, though, is make requests to somebody above my level in government. For instance, I was getting lousy answers on an airline problem, so I had to say, 'Bill, you must telephone the Secretary. We can't resolve it without his help.' Administrative assistants do not telephone cabinet members!"

Thompson feels "called" to his work on Capitol Hill, but "disagrees with liberal preachers who are 'looking to the politicians to get this country out of a hole.' " The gospel of Jesus can't be identified with any political, economic, or sociological system, he insists.

Dr. Robert Andringa is one of about 1,800 persons who do research and draft legislation for the committees and subcommittees of the Senate and House on Capitol Hill. Well-paid and highly influential, the committee staffers are sometimes called a "third house of Congress."

A slim dark-haired scholar with an avid interest in higher education, Andringa directs a staff of sixteen responsible to the Republican congressmen on the Education and Labor Committee. The twenty-two Democratic committee members have a staff of sixty-five. Together, the eighty-one staffers handle all labor and education bills, from minimum wage laws and school lunch programs to special education for older Americans.

"If we make an issue partisan we lose every time from the Republican point of view," Andringa says. "We're outnumbered. So we have to try harder, get better data, seek more outside expertise, give each issue some nonpartisan credibility."

Andringa has had "tempting offers to leave, including a college presidency," but feels his job as a committee staff man is "the most challenging at this time." As an administrator he recruits and hires new employees and keeps staffers "responding and available to the Republican committee members." He also attends conferences and seminars "to keep abreast of the latest research," delivers speeches, and outlines speeches for his congressmen.

The Michigan educator "grew up" in a Methodist church but "didn't think in terms of a personal commitment" until he was approached by a Campus Crusade for Christ staffer when a sophomore at Michigan State. While there Andringa was invited to the National Prayer Breakfast in Washington, where Doug Coe introduced him to Rep. Albert Quie. "Mr. Quie asked me about my job plans," he recalls. "I said I was interested in college administration. He said, 'Government is involved in that. Why don't you try it for a year and find out what Congress is like?' During that first year [1964], I met with golfer Jim Hiskey and others in a prayer group. I came back every year after that until I got my doctorate in '67. Two years later I took a staff job on Capitol Hill."

Andringa recalls that the first bill he worked on took two-and-one-half years to pass. "There were 300 differences within the House and Senate. Each had to be discussed and reconciled.

"Every day you're trying to reconcile views. You have to learn to disagree agreeably and not carry over your feelings to the next day. Being a Christian helps you keep cool and act as a minister of reconciliation. Christianity here is not pie in the sky, but salt as you show evidence of love."

The "salt" of Christian witness and influence is spread all across Washington. Besides the Christians on congressional, judicial, and White House staffs, thousands more work beside dedicated, conscientious non-Christians within the eleven sprawling cabinet departments and fifty independent agencies and commissions. Controversial columnist Jack Anderson, who admits lambasting the bureaucracy for "inefficiency, red tape, fumbling and—on occasion —corruption," concedes that "the preponderance of civil servants are diligent, trustworthy, intelligent people who really believe that public service is a public trust. They are making the system work."

Dr. Betsy Ancker-Johnson, assistant secretary of Commerce for Science and Technology, and once a college staffer for Inter-Varsity Christian Fellowship in California, must be included in Anderson's preponderance. One of the three highest ranking women in government at the time of her appointment by President Nixon in 1973,* Dr.

*The other two at the time were Anne L. Armstrong, a presidential counselor and Dixie Lee Ray, chairman of the Atomic Energy Commission.

Ancker-Johnson is chief advisor on science and technology to the Secretary of Commerce and oversees 7,000 employees and the $200 million combined budget of the National Bureau of Standards, Patent Office, Office of Telecommunications, National Technical Information Service, Office of Environmental Affairs, and Office of Product Standards.

As an appointee who serves "at the pleasure of the President," she observes candidly that the President's "pleasure" could be withdrawn "tomorrow." The average tenure of her office is twenty-two months. No mere "token" female, Dr. Ancker-Johnson has impressive credentials. They include important research, teaching, management experience, and a Ph.D. magna cum laude in physics from renowned Tuebingen University in Germany. Her specialty was the study of nuclear energy for peacetime use. Before coming to Washington she managed a task force for the Boeing Company studying a concept for an institute that would concentrate on coping with world needs.

Dr. Ancker-Johnson is a committed follower of Jesus Christ. "I became a Christian in high school, but really discovered what it was all about during a course in biblical history at Wellesley College. Writing a term paper on the mission of Jesus proved to be a turning point for me. I just couldn't see how you could be intellectually honest and not at least admit that Jesus claimed to come from God. Either you believe or you don't."

While she considers her spiritual home to be "still very much with Inter-Varsity," her church home in the Washington area is McClean Presbyterian Church, which she attends with her husband Harold (a professor of mathematics in a local college) and four school-age daughters. On the subject of personal home life, she observes: "People must wonder how I can be subject to my husband, as the Bible says, and do all these jobs assigned to me. But it seems to me God was simply stating a fact about the way men and women are put together. Obviously there are differences in the sexes—and aren't we glad there are! This has never been an issue in our marriage and family. What first attracted me to my husband was that he took for granted that I was as interested in electrons as he was in differential geometry. That had nothing to do with whether I would be a good wife and mother. But I must say I have sensed a feeling in some organized Christian groups that [because of my career interests] there must really be something wrong with me.

"Let's face it, if you're the only woman giving a scientific paper to a thousand men, you stand out. It's a syndrome that becomes very uncomfortable. It's like being a Christian in a secular place. You get the feeling that everybody is watching you because you are a Christian. But what is there to be afraid of? You know you're in His hands, so you go on and do your thing. All that really matters is that He understands—and forgives when you err."

Dr. Ancker-Johnson believes that American leaders will need extra confidence and courage in facing national problems, the most serious of which she thinks is energy. "The next two decades are going to be very critical to our history. We don't have enough supply of energy to continue at the rate of growth we've had. We have been using energy at an increasing rate of about 4 percent a year and there is a close relationship between unemployment and energy. We may have some severe poverty, tremendous dislocations in our society, and some tremendous battles over whether we are going to sort of rape our land in strip-mining coal to maintain a level of energy use. This is going to call for some very levelheaded thinking. It's a time when I'm glad to be a Christian.

"Really, I think we Christians have such a distinct advantage over people who are insecure, worried, and uptight all the time. I see that all over Washington. People afraid to make decisions, for example. If you have a sense of belonging to God, you just have a certain extra confidence and courage. That doesn't mean you don't make mistakes. Usually you can fix those up. One of the really great things about being a Christian is the assurance that you belong to the Creator of the universe, and He has this great master plan, and it's all going to work out one way or another."

Another top official with similar views is Richard Wiley, the

Nixon-appointed chairman of the powerful—and sometimes controversial—Federal Communications Commission (FCC). A Methodist, Wiley says: "I have to feel God has given me these opportunities. I am not, however, a Calvinist in the sense that I can just sit back and believe God will do it all. Being a Christian does have a bearing on the way you conduct yourself in everyday work and relationships. My faith affects everything I do, the way I treat other people, the way I handle issues."

The FCC has 1,840 employees, and both its responsibilities and powers to regulate the broadcast industry are awesome. Within the limits of law and court decisions, the FCC can fine a station or network for violations, close a station down by failing to renew its license, or refuse an application for a new license.

"We fined a station in a Chicago suburb several thousand dollars for broadcasting what we considered incedent programs," states Wiley, a lawyer who formerly served as the FCC's general counsel. "A court test of this [case] may provide some guidelines as to whether there can be a different standard on something that comes into the home where a child can simply turn it on and something which consenting adults can pay money to see in a theater."

Having Christian convictions and four children, Wiley is naturally concerned about broadcast morality. "But whatever my personal views might be," he says, "we are proscribed from censoring unless under federal law the program is indecent, obscene, or profane. I don't think FCC has the power that a lot of people think we have. Let us say that a section of 'Maude' was called 'improper.' We have to be very careful that the FCC doesn't set itself up as an arbitrator or a truth-in-decency proprietor. We are charged only with carrying out the dictates of Federal law."

A second common complaint received by the FCC relates to a station broadcasting only one side of a controversial issue. The majority of religious broadcasters have experienced no trouble with the FCC, but a few that blended religion and politics have had widely publicized hassles with the government regulatory agency, mostly over the issue of fairness.

"A broadcaster is a public trustee," says Wiley. "We expect him to make a profit, but he can't use his station as a pet toy. The fairness doctrine requires him to give reasonable time to contrasting views on controversial issues of public importance."

Wiley, who describes himself as a "concerned, committed layman," called on some 1,000 religious broadcasters at their 1974 Washington convention to use their "electric pulpits" to reach the unchurched and "those who do not know the Lord" rather than using their radio time primarily for fund-raising. Wiley himself has preached in his church and participated in lay evangelistic visitation.

The FCC chairman advises citizens offended by specific programs to complain first to their local broadcaster. "A station isn't simply a spigot for a network. It must make decisions on the basis of community needs. Then if the local station doesn't provide a hearing or satisfaction, the complaint should come to us."

The FCC's counterpart in the world of high finance is the Securities and Exchange Commission, set up after the 1929 stock market crash to protect investors against deception in money markets. Paul Glenn, a tall, blue-eyed Christian Missionary Alliance Sunday-school teacher with modishly long hair, is a young attorney-investigator and one of 1,670 SEC employees. Glenn holds that "while morality can't be legislated, we must make it an issue. Our laws that are based on the Ten Commandments are guidelines to help make people act morally. However, I don't think the answer lies so much in the role a person is in, as in the person himself. No matter where you are you can violate the law."

The thrust of SEC protection "is to determine that investors get all the information needed to make up their own minds," Glenn says. "If they make bad investments then, it is their own fault."

It is only when there is suspicion that facts are being withheld or not being stated properly in interstate financing that SEC investigators like Paul Glenn step in to check on possible violations.

One of Glenn's assignments called for the investigation of a multimillion-dollar bond issue offered by a large Baptist congregation in an eastern state. The church was using the money to finance expansion of its educational facilities and radio outreach. Glenn and two other SEC operatives checked church financial records and determined that on the basis of current income and expense it could not meet the bond obligations. They also concluded that prospective investors had not been adequately informed about the church's financial condition.

The pastor and other leaders contested bitterly the SEC's case against the church (Glenn was seen by some members as "a tool of Satan"), alleging the SEC's requirements regarding church bond sales were unfair. Nevertheless, the findings of Glenn and his colleagues resulted in a court-appointed committee of five nonmember local businessmen to oversee church expenditures and to safeguard investor interests. The committee made the church cut back some of its holdings and programs, causing more anguish. But before Glenn left he was thanked by the church's chief financial officer for, in effect, helping them stave off complete bankruptcy.

Glenn believes he acted as his job required. "I wasn't influenced by any extra compassion just because they were my evangelical brothers," he says. "But on the other hand I wasn't disillusioned over what they had done. I felt they were sincere. The mistakes weren't intentional." He insists that the SEC does not discriminate against churches. "They have the same responsibilities as any other group in offering investments to the public."

Another Washington Christian committed to both his work and his Lord is James Koan, a traffic engineering specialist for the Department of Transportation (DOT), an agency responsible for developing national policies to provide "fast, safe, efficient, convenient, and economical transportation." Koan, who once worked on a U.S. Agency for International Development road-building project in Cambodia, believes it is "easy to lose your identity" in a large government bureaucracy that had 71,382 employees in 1974. "The prayer groups have helped tremendously at this point," he says. "In them I rub shoulders with brothers and sisters of all levels in

DOT. All of us are the same rank around the cross and we really value one another as Christian persons."

Koan, a Baptist Sunday school superintendent, says his faith has given him a deep sense of accomplishment in his government work. "The Lord definitely led me to come here where I could help with serious environmental problems." As an example, he recalls that in 1968 he and several other engineers suggested that a lane in an urban-area expressway be reserved during the morning and afternoon rush hours for buses and pool cars. A pilot test on Interstate 95 between suburban Virginia and downtown Washington has proven the idea's worth. Today, buses and pool cars carrying thousands of commuters zip along I-95 past miles of slow-moving—and sometimes stalled—autos, many of them with only one occupant. Koan thinks nation-wide adoption of this traffic incentive would help ease the energy crunch, reduce congestion, and result in tremendous improvement of air quality.

George Brandt, an attorney, is a highway safety management specialist for DOT. A Sunday school teacher at National Presbyterian Church, the husky six-footer is a thoughtful man who "wants to help make the system work." He is presently trying to help unclog courts in cities across the country.

"Traffic makes up 80 percent of the cases that come before metro lower courts," he explains. "We'd like to see license bureaus handle routine traffic cases. This would free the judges to work on more serious cases, but this must be done within local jurisdictions. We can only make suggestions and provide information on what various states are doing.

Brandt worked in county and state government in Oregon before coming to Washington. "There is this 'I'll scratch your back if you'll scratch mine' principle operating at all stages of government," he says candidly. "At every level you have a power structure buried in the bureaucracy. Washington just has many more layers of bureaucracy.

"A government worker must make a conscious effort to bring moral judgment into play. It's easy to slide, to take the route of expediency. What happens is that you start developing your work the best you can. Then you find people who don't want what you want or they want it for themselves. If you present your idea, there's a bureaucratic struggle of who's in charge. If you leave it to the group it may never get done because it's so hard to get a consensus. What is desperately needed is close understanding and support of one another, just plain old trust and faith—which I've found to be a byproduct of Christianity."

Across the Potomac at the Pentagon, Colonel Arthur G. Dewey is another who believes that Christian faith can lift morale in a government agency. The former White House Fellow believes that the key to effectiveness is servanthood. "Denying yourself gives you a fantastic advantage in getting things done in this town where so many are trying to advance themselves. One who wants to serve and has established his credentials can become almost indispensable."

A West Pointer with a Master's degree, Dewey is a slightly-built, think-tank type. As a White House Fellow he was one of about 15 selected from 2,000 applicants to take special high-level assignments of strategic importance. He was assigned to a small task force charged with mediation of the two sides during the bitter 1967-9 Nigerian civil war. "I saw God change personalities in ways that can't be rationally explained," he recalls.

Dewey doesn't see any conflict between Christian faith and present national policy. Nor does he believe the U.S. commitment of Viet Nam was "morally wrong," although he admits "some errors in judgment were made."

He disagrees with pacifist proposals for disarmament. "One has to accept the essential sinfulness of man. You cannot totally disarm and have a stable world. But it's a very popular idea that man is perfectable. That's why a lot of foundation money goes into peace studies and very little into strategic studies which recognizes the need for a strong defense."

As might be expected, John Broger, director of Information and Education for the Armed Forces, lines up with Dewey on the need for a strong defense. The Pentagon isn't known for harboring pacifists. But Broger believes that the two and one quarter million members of the armed services need much more than military training. Says Broger: "These people serve at possible risk of life. They need a spiritual foundation."

Broger does not see religious and moral training of service personnel as an issue of church-state. "I don't want anyone telling me what I must believe, how I must live, or when I must worship. But by the same token, if you separate every single spiritual quality and standard of morality from government, you have chaos."

A twenty-year veteran with the Defense Department, Broger administers a billion-dollar budget in his department. A map of the world frames one wall of his large studio-office; opposite it is a broadcasting console that is tied to a worldwide satellite communication system.

He briskly ticks off the responsibilities of his department: overseeing 1,100 radio stations, 1,200 periodicals, 1,900 troop newspapers, forty or fifty motion pictures a year plus other audio visuals, and absentee voting for military personnel.

Broger's pilot project of one-minute radio spot announcements that invite service personnel with problems to call a hot-line number got under way in June 1974. "We want to orient callers to think of the Bible as a resource," he explains. "We want them to counsel with lay people, then become related to a Bible study group of their peers."

Broger is not disturbed over possible criticism that he is using his office to propagate the Bible as columnist Jack Anderson once accused him. "This is only one part of our total educational program. We do thousands of spots on other subjects: savings bonds, re-enlistment, drug and alcohol abuse, insurance, environment, ecology, and every other conceivable subject a person in the military should be conscious of. We aren't saying that the Bible is the only spiritual approach, but that it is an important resource tool."

Broger is a former missionary who co-founded the independent Far East Broadcasting Company, a mission agency which blankets the world with Christian programs in many languages.

One's faith and vocation are integrally related, Broger believes. He rejects the compartmentalist view that one serves Caesar part-time and God part-time. "I serve the Lord full-time and our armed forces as well," he insists. "There are plenty of Scriptures to validate that concept. Either you are serving God or you are not. You're in full-time service for God, with all of your life committed to Him, or you are really not committed to Him at all."

The same sense of commitment marks two strategically placed evangelicals in the State Department's Agency for International Development (AID).

James Cudney is an evaluation officer for security assistance. He travels in six nations that receive American security aid: Thailand, Cambodia, Laos, Israel, Jordan, and Egypt. Before leaving on a round-the-world trip, Cudney asks the Fellowship House for a list of contacts in the countries he will be visiting. Some may be national Christians who need encouragement, others non-Christians who need friendship and knowledge of the Gospel. In 1974 he participated in the Philippines National Prayer Breakfast in Manila, which drew 700 national Filipino leaders.

Cleo Shook is associate director of AID's Population and Humanitarian Assistance Bureau, working in the office of Private and Voluntary Cooperation. He has a hand in the administration of some $240 million of U.S. foreign aid funds. A large part of this is funneled in cash grants to 119 voluntary service organizations, which include many Christian mission groups, doing relief and rehabilitation projects overseas. He has had many opportunities to talk with national leaders abroad, as an Army officer, Peace Corps director in Iran, deputy director for AID in Northeast Asia and the Philippines, and in his present work with humanitarian agencies.

After army service in Asia, where he was General George C. Marshall's signal officer, Shook signed a contract in 1953 with the Afghanistan government to become head of the mechanical engineering department at its Institute of Technology. A year later the Afghan government asked AID to take over the institute. One of the new arriving AID teachers was Cudney, a former cameraman and lighting director for NBC television in Chicago. They shared the same evangelical faith and have been close friends ever since.

Shook, Cudney, and a half dozen other teachers worked and lived with some 200 Afghan students. They took care of the students when they were ill, counseled them about personal problems, and tutored at night those needing special academic help. Though Shook and Cudney were both zealous Christians, they could not evangelize because conversion was strictly forbidden by Afghan law. They could only communicate their faith through love.

In the years since many of the students have gained influential positions in Afghan society. Some have come to Washington and dropped by Cudney and Shook's offices to thank them with tears in their eyes for what they did in the institute.

At home in Washington Shook is an elder and Sunday-school teacher at Barcroft Bible Church in suburban Virginia. Cudney is a deacon at Fourth Presbyterian Church. Both are active in State Department prayer groups.

The Christians who serve as "ambassadors for Christ" are to be found in all segments of government. Some additional examples:

Jack Allen trims congressional locks in the House of Representatives barber shop. A fellow barber took him to the special Inaugural worship service held for President Lyndon Johnson at the National City Christian Church. The featured speaker was Billy Graham. His forceful message started Allen to thinking in lines that led to his conversion a month later. Then Bob Harrington, the colorful "chaplain of Bourbon Street," came along and challenged him to tell his customers about Christ. This he continues to do.

William "Fish-Bait" Miller was doorkeeper for the House of Representatives until 1975. ("Down on the Mississippi Gulf coast where I grew up," he recalls, "I was so sickly as a child that folks didn't think I was good for much but bait. They called me 'Shrimp Bait,' 'Lobster Bait,' and 'Fish Bait,' and as I grew older the last name stuck.") His "mis-tuh Speak-uh, the Pres-i-dent of the U-nited States," introduced chief executives to all joint gatherings of Congress for over thirty years. The legendary Miller, who once told England's visiting Prince Philip that he "was the handsomest brute we'd ever seen," is Sunday school superintendent at Memorial Baptist Church in Arlington, Virginia.

Fred Rhodes, another leading Baptist layman, is director of the Postal Rate Commission. Converted at age 38 in a noonday service led by Billy Graham, Rhodes tells his men's Sunday school class that religion is a seven-day-a-week affair and that Sunday church services are just a "service station" to provide spiritual fuel and inspiration as they "live and witness" their faith during the week.

Dr. Jean Adams, a microbiologist with the U.S. Department of Agriculture, is a lay leader among Baptist women of Washington.

Major Gene Arnold, a Marine historian, is active at National Presbyterian Church.

Paul Liberman, an executive in the Department of Commerce, is president of the Washington Messianic-Jewish Alliance.

Richard Schubert, a leader in the Nazarene Church, is Under Secretary of Labor.

The Honorable George Powell, Trial Judge with the National Labor Relations Board, participates in Fellowship House ministries.

Homer McMurray, a clerk who records debates in the House of Representatives, is a leader in Capitol Hill prayer groups.

Lt. Commander Stephen Harris is assigned to Naval Intelligence in Washington. Harris commanded the intelligence operation aboard the ill-fated spy ship *Pueblo* and also led Protestant services for the crew before capture. His book *My Anchor Held* (Fleming H. Revell Publishers) recounts the spiritual experiences of the *Pueblo* prisoners in North Korea. A Harvard graduate who attends Fourth Presbyterian Church, he is also a leader in the Officer's Christian Fellowship and a popular speaker among Washington church groups.

In a chat with a reporter about to embark on a series of

interviews with Washington Christians, Harris remarked: "You'll find this old government isn't in such bad hands after all."

CHAPTER TEN

Women in Washington

It is no secret that the strains and exhaustive work hours in high office take a heavy toll on marriage and family. In the 92nd Congress, for instance, five legislators from Michigan alone, with seventeen children among them, were divorced. Six weeks before filing for dissolution of her marriage, a senator's wife from another state expressed openly the sad lot of many political wives opting for divorce. She had no life of her own, felt trapped and disillusioned, and seldom saw her glamorous husband. He could have his power and prestige all by himself, she said.

The divorces and separations, however, are only part of the story. Unhappy and strained marriages abound, with some high officeholders trying to hold their homes together for little more than image-protection reasons. Barbara Howar, the caustic Washington writer and television hostess, observes that "by and large, wife-changing and high office are not compatible."[1]

A wife may become bitter and blame marriage miseries on the political vocation. She may sulk at home, hoping for his political defeat, while he hits the campaign trail. She may seethe in silence, hoping that somehow he will come to his senses before their marriage goes over the cliff. More likely, in devotion to her husband, she will play out her role in frustrated and painful acquiescence. Along the way, she may seek psychiatric help in a valiant effort to keep her balance.

The higher her husband's star ascends, the more difficult this may be.

Few long-term Washington political wives have been without trauma. Betty Ford, who is the admiration of many women for her emotional balance and happy marriage, has openly told reporters about once seeing a psychiatrist due to a pinched nerve and tension. During this time she was caring for her four children while her congressman husband was busy with office duties and making speeches. His schedule was so packed that his secretary frequently came to the Ford home in Alexandria, Virginia, to pick up clean clothes for him. In a *McCall's* magazine article Mrs. Ford recalled that the psychiatrist has suggested that "I shouldn't give up everything for Jerry and the children, that I had to also think about things that mattered to me."[2] The same article quotes Mr. Ford's brother, Tom, as saying that the then congressional leader had a "guilt complex about it," and tried to help by staying home from speaking engagements, massaging her neck, bringing her gifts, and helping out in whatever way he could. In time the emotional pressures were eased, but Mrs. Ford reportedly still suffers physical pain from the pinched nerve. The difficulty has apparently brought the family closer together. Mrs. Ford's 1974 cancer surgery, during which she reportedly came to a "real awakening" and discovered she "really was a child of Christ," has brought the Fords closer.

Perhaps no woman better understands the sacrifice required of the political wife than Joan Kennedy. At the birth of her first child in 1960, fifteen months after marriage to the youngest of the Kennedy brothers, she reportedly said: "All I want is to be a happy wife and mother."

The series of family tragedies, now legendary, that made her senator husband a national figure have eroded this dream. The last was the shattering discovery that her twelve-year-old son, Teddy, had cancer of the bone marrow and had to have his right leg removed. Even while she tried to help him adjust to the trauma, she herself was the prisoner of her husband's gazing public. At the hospital she was constantly in the limelight as people would recognize her and ask questions. As one of her friends explained to writer Kandy Stroud, "She'd have to greet them and be pleasant, no matter how she felt inside. She told me she felt she was constantly on display. She could never just be a mother alone with her sick child."[3]

There are scores of wives of lesser known political luminaries who have been injured by the wedge which the demands of high office can drive into a marriage. Often a husband may not know how much his career has cost his family relationships until too late.

"One of the great problems of political leadership is to wake up in middle life and find your family gone," says Harold Hughes, who has tried to help save many marriages. "A man has been sleeping with a woman for thirty years and finds he doesn't know her or the children she has birthed. It's critically important that the family pray together and share common problems." Fortunately for his family, Hughes saw the potential dangers early in his political career. While he was governor of Iowa he refused all Sunday speaking engagements, even at churches, so his family could be together.

"It's very hard to be a good father and husband and a good congressman, because the job is so complex," acknowledges Rep. Charles Bennett, who has three children at home. "You don't have time unless you make time. For many years I've set aside Friday nights for my family. I don't do anything else on that night, unless there's nothing I can do with them. Then on Sundays we go to church together."

Walter Fauntroy voices the same concern. "Yesterday afternoon, my ten-year-old son called me about four o'clock to come and play catch with him. I had two receptions to attend, but I just decided they would have to miss me. That may not sound like the Christian thing to do when people are expecting you. But I felt I had to say no."

Cooperation and understanding on the part of the husband helps. But the pressures upon him invariably force the wife to bear the greater burden of adjustment. She must often find her own meaningful purpose for living.

Many Washington political wives are finding this through

Bible studies and prayer groups held apart from the rush and pressures of political activity.

One is Irene Conlan, wife of Rep. John Conlan and the mother of two preschool sons. Trim as a model and tanned, with soft brown eyes and dark hair combed straight back, she holds no illusions about the life of a congressman's wife.

"We have two homes, with each one being just a base for John where he temporarily parks his hat. When Congress is in session John goes home at least every third weekend and during heavy periods he's gone every week. It's a shame while our boys are so little, but we both feel we are where the Lord wants us."

Married only since 1969, the Conlans met when John was a state senator and Irene director of nursing at St. Luke's Hospital in Phoenix. Perhaps because both are committed Christians, she has been pleasantly surprised by life in Washington.

"I found the city to be very friendly and most congressional wives down to earth, not social climbers as I had thought they might be. Those I know are sharp, but they are home oriented. They know how to work and sacrifice from having helped their husbands in public office. They know how to manage because they've had to do all the home managing when their husbands are gone. They are a delightful group."

Mrs. Conlan even finds Washington "less hectic" than Phoenix. "There I represent John everywhere I go because I am his wife. I am expected to appear at a great number of affairs. Here I am sort of lost in the big crowd. I completely skip the cocktail circuit, which isn't my thing anyway. I just go to the affairs John thinks are important, and I never go more than three times a week. Some weeks, I don't have to go out at night at all.

"When I first came I did worry a little about fitting into the role of a congressman's wife. Then I decided that I am me and they would just have to take me as I am. I have an aversion to phoniness. Any question that has to do with me I answer straight. If it's political, I try not to speak at all. I may have to say on an issue, 'I don't know John's reaction but this is my opinion.' People like for you to be yourself.

"Most of the time here I can be a simple little housewife and mother. I think that's the most fantastic thing in life. It was a joke among my friends in Arizona that I went barefoot. They said now that you're going to be somebody, you'll have to wear shoes. I don't have to for we live in a very informal neighborhood."

One day Mrs. Conlan visited a home Bible-study group in a Virginia suburb, led by Eleanor Page, an army officer's widow associated with Campus Crusade for Christ. "Eleanor's Bible study on the mystique of womanhood was so exciting that I asked if she could come over here and start one for congressional wives. I called the wives of freshman congressmen whom I knew, and to be sure of a good attendance invited some military wives also. After a few weeks we had so many that the group divided, with the congressional wives staying at our house and the military gals going to another place.

"The biblical teaching that a wife is to submit to her husband and let him be the head of the family is enough to throw Women's Lib into a tizzy," Mrs. Conlan says, "but it has sure improved a lot of marriages around here. I don't know of any woman who has taken the course that is not more deeply in love with her husband. And some of those who once weren't enthusiastic about political life are now going back to the districts to help their husbands get reelected. One woman whose husband's chances for reelection were very poor in 1974 said that if she were not sent to Washington for anything else, this course was worth it."

In addition to the congressional wives, the group at the Conlan home has included Julie Nixon Eisenhower and the wife of a high White House aide in the Nixon administration. Both professed faith in Christ as a result of the home Bible study.

In 1974 a second Bible course, "Ten Basic Steps to Christian Maturity," published by Campus Crusade, was taught by Eleanor Page in Mrs. Conlan's home. By summer the group grew to twenty-five and decided to divide again. Mrs. Conlan anticipated that within a few months some of the members would begin teaching in other homes.

The groups sparked by Eleanor Page and Irene Conlan are
Janes-come-lately compared to the large congressional wives
group which meets biweekly in Fellowship House. This group
began in 1961 when Alicia Abrahamsen (Abraham Vereide's
daughter) and Marian Adair (wife of Rep. Ross Adair from
Indiana) planned the first women's prayer breakfast in
Washington. It was held at the same time and in the same
building as the National Prayer Breakfast. After speaking to
the larger group, President John F. Kennedy slipped out and
greeted the women assembled in a nearby banquet room.

Six years later Mrs. Abrahamsen began the congressional
wives prayer group. It met in Senate committee rooms before
moving to Fellowship House in 1972.

This group is structured and has officers, but no regular
teacher. The president for 1974 was Mrs. James A. McClure,
wife of the junior senator from Idaho, and the program
chairwoman was Mrs. Frank Horton, whose husband
represents the thirty-fourth district of New York.

Usually from twenty-five to forty wives attend the
meetings, which are held every first and third Thursday of
the month from 10 A.M. through lunch when Congress is in
session. During election years the last meeting is held in June
so those whose husbands are running again can campaign.

At the June 1974 session the wives of retiring legislators,
including Mrs. Sam Ervin, were given a farewell. Pastor
Louis Evans of National Presbyterian Church was guest
speaker.

With Watergate heavy on everyone's mind, he gave a
dramatic portrayal of possible responses Adam might have
made to God after eating the forbidden fruit:

"I could bluff it and pretend there's nothing different.

I could blame it on the woman, and say it was her fault.

I could run away and hide.

I could say, 'I goofed, Lord, forgive me!'"

Evans concluded by suggesting it was always best to
honestly face up to mistakes, ask God's forgiveness, then
begin anew.

The "prompter" behind the scenes of the congressional
wives prayer group is Fellowship House associate Barbara

Priddy. Miss Priddy, the fortyish, attractive brunette who succeeded Alicia Abrahamsen as leader of the women's work, counts six women who "came to know Christ in 1974." She senses "increased warmth and love developing among the women, many of whom were long-time church members but who had never experienced the personal reality of Christ before coming to Washington. Mrs. Horton, our program chairman, is a good example," she notes. "In the group she saw that her churchgoing had been a form without the Spirit."

Miss Priddy understands the special circumstances which envelop the congressional wife. "Whether in Washington or back in the home district her husband is under tremendous time pressure. His schedule allows them little time for real communication. Here in Washington there's a constant round of activities. She's torn whether to be with him or home with the children. There's also the competitiveness of political life, which I don't think the women feel as keenly as the men. But it still affects the women. I think of three wives whose husbands were defeated after long careers in Congress. Two tended to become bitter, but one, after a family tragedy, turned to the Lord and found healing. She was able to stand up and share this with the group. The Lord has done beautiful things through her."

Prayer groups and breakfasts for wives of officials have been organized in several states, according to Miss Priddy. Fourteen hundred came to the June 1973 prayer breakfast hosted by Mrs. Otis R. Bowen, wife of the Indiana governor. Three hundred attended a prayer brunch sponsored by Governor Reubin Askew's wife in Tallahassee, Florida, in April 1974. At the conclusion Mrs. Askew invited everyone to come to the governor's mansion and pray with her every Tuesday morning.

Besides the congressional wives group that meets at Fellowship House, other women's groups originally started by Alicia Abrahamsen still meet across the Washington area. One is in the Pentagon, another in the State Department. A home group is composed of wives whose husbands work for the Department of Interior. Another home group includes wives of husbands in the U.S. Foreign Service. A woman who became a Christian in this group started several German groups when her husband was transferred to Frankfurt. And still more women's prayer groups have been started by such chain reactions elsewhere in the world.

One of the least known Washington women's groups resulted from two press wives praying together over their mutual problems (adjustments of living in Washington, husbands working long and erratic hours, and the like). They felt the need of a larger circle but didn't know how or where to begin.

One of the two was Mrs. Forrest (Verma) Boyd, whose spouse is the White House correspondent for the Mutual Broadcasting System. On Easter Sunday, 1971, when her husband was among the White House Press Corps with the Nixon family in Florida, she and her three teen-agers were late for services at Fourth Presbyterian. It was raining hard, and she dropped the children off in front of the church, then had to park five blocks away. She was sloshing back to the church through puddles when a car stopped and a smiling woman offered her a ride. It was Barbara Priddy, the very person she needed to meet.

The media wives group continues to meet each Wednesday afternoon in Verma Boyd's home under Barbara Priddy's leadership. Ten to twelve American and foreign wives participate. Like other groups, they pray for individual needs, their families and husbands, and national leaders in government.

No one in the White House knew about the press wives' group until early 1974. Miss Priddy was there for a tea and in conversation with Mrs. Nixon mentioned that many womens' groups around the city were praying for her, her husband, and the country. The First Lady smiled her appreciation, then added, "Well, someday we're going to get them to pray for the press, aren't we?"

"You'll be glad to know," Miss Priddy replied, "that several press wives—some have husbands in the White House Press Corps—already pray this way."

Mrs. Nixon seemed impressed.

The former First Lady later gave permission for a women's prayer group to meet in the White House East Wing, beginning in April 1974. However, she chose not to attend.

This group started much as the media wives' group, when two women discovered they had mutual spiritual interests. Joyce Adams, receptionist for VIP's, and Jan Ingersoll, assistant to the director of the White House Social Protocol Office, then sent a questionnaire to women employees they thought might be interested, asking for opinions and time preferences.

Ten came for the first 7:30 A.M. meeting in the Family Theater, where the Presidential family and guests view movies. They agreed that the group "could not belong to any one person. Jesus Christ will be our one and only Leader, and the Bible will be studied as the only recognized Word of God," they said in a letter to all White House women employees.

One of the ten knew Eleanor Page and suggested her as a teacher. Mrs. Page taught her course on womanly mystique. When this study was completed, a program committee began inviting outside speakers to come and tell about their faith. After only two months so many White House women were coming that a second group was started in the Executive Office Building next door to the White House.

A sixteen-year White House career employee, Miss Ingersoll attended a mixed prayer group of men and women during the Johnson Administration. "But Washington is just now coming alive for the Lord," she believes.

Joyce Adams is a presidential appointee, as is her husband Wayne, an executive in the General Services Administration. She is considering writing a book entitled "Coffee, Tea, or Christ?" based upon her experiences as an airline hostess and a receptionist at the White House.

"I felt I was strong in my relationship with Christ before we started our group," she says. "Now I'm even stronger for I know I'm not by myself."

There are many more women's prayer groups in residential areas of Washington and the suburbs. Some are sponsored by churches, others appear to be unsponsored and unstructured. Wives of well-known Washington personalities are involved. For example, Mrs. Charles Colson finds spiritual support in a McClean, Virginia, group, as does Mrs. Jeb Magruder in a group sponsored by National Presbyterian Church. Mrs. Dean Rusk, wife of the former Secretary of State, and her daughter pray and study the Bible with a group in Quantico, Virginia. Most women in the prayer groups, however, are as little known as their housewife counterparts in other metropolitan areas of the country.

"We don't seek publicity," Joyce Adams stresses. "Many don't attend church and the prayer group is the only religious experience they have all week. We don't want people coming to watch. We want other Christians to know only because we need their prayers."

"With everything that's coming to light in politics, Washington women are realizing answers are not where they have been looking," observes Irene Conlan. "Many have been going to church all their lives without ever hearing of a personal relationship with Jesus Christ. Not ever. When they find that this is possible, they are overwhelmed and immediately start bringing their friends. That's why these Bible studies and prayer groups are catching on so fast. If Watergate hasn't done any other thing, it has made these women want something really meaningful."

CHAPTER ELEVEN

Strategies for Ministry

Burnett Thompson, the Methodist minister who has found a "calling" as a congressional administrative aide, was enthusiastically telling a visiting clergyman about the various prayer groups among government people. When Thompson finished, the minister asked airily, "How does all this fit in with the church?"

With a few notable exceptions, the churches and denominational groups in the Washington area have had little to do with the spreading prayer-group movement. "It's a shame, but it's true," notes UPI reporter Wesley Pippert, himself a licensed lay Methodist minister. "The groups are carried on almost in spite of the churches around town."

Another Washington observer, who has been involved with both the Washington prayer groups and church congregations, goes further: "Denominationally competitive ministers around here are one of the greatest blocks to a supernatural, Holy Spirit awakening among masses of government people. They feel threatened by indigenous, spontaneous movements not under their purview or control. They zealously try to protect their own little kingdoms."

Harsh overstatements perhaps. In all fairness, many pastors simply did not know of the prayer group movement until the spate of national publicity. It is largely a lay-led movement, and its members have not sought publicity—even in their churches. Also, the average pastor is kept so busy with the housekeeping work of his own church that he can ill afford to get involved in yet another project—a transdenominational one, at that. And because of the press of the work and needs in his own community or church he may not readily see Washington and its environs as the "greater parish" or, in Baptist parlance, "mission field." While some lay leaders wish more pastors would give an assist from time to time (such as providing names or encouraging church members who are federal employees to participate in groups), most count it a blessing that pastors have not become involved. Among other things, the lay leaders fear the presence of pastors coming to the groups would inhibit discussion, lead to an emphasis on structure and programs, and ignite doctrinal controversies.

As in other major American cities, Christianity in Washington is splintered into a variety of denominations. Dr. Caspar Nannes, former long-time religion editor of the *Washington Star-News,* estimates there are 1,200 churches in the Washington metro area of 2.8 million people. These include the cultic and exotic, but mostly are mainline Protestant and Catholic, with more Episcopalian, Christian Scientist, and Unitarian-Universalist congregations than are found in many other urban areas.

The older churches are rich in history. For example, George Washington and Robert E. Lee worshiped in Pews 60 and 46 respectively in the old red-brick Christ Church that stands among tombstones dating from colonial times in Alexandria, Virginia.

Some of the newer houses of worship are showplaces of architecture for the 18 million tourists who pour into Washington each year. The $20 million Washington (Episcopal) Cathedral, still unfinished, is the most popular attraction. A close competitor is the new seven-story, windowless Mormon Temple made of glistening white Alabama marble, from which six shimmering spires reach more than 200 feet skyward. Atop the tallest is a two-and-half ton figure of the angel Moroni blowing a golden trumpet. (No tourists are allowed inside; the temple is reserved for Mormons engaging in certain rites.)

Few tourists see the hundreds of neighborhood and suburban churches which rank-and-file Washingtonians frequent. According to Dr. Nannes, who has visited scores of them, they are well-attended, and many have two services to accommodate the crowds.

The distinctly evangelical churches, where Bible teaching is emphasized, seem to be thriving—especially in the over 200 bedroom communities that surround the city of Washington. For example, Redland (Southern) Baptist, near Rockville, Maryland, grew in six years from six members to more than 600 in 1974, with half being government workers.

Redland's pastor Bob Rich, who came from Abilene, Texas, had to adapt his ministry to the Washington life style. "We had to condense our program," he says. "Life is faster here. People get home later and travel a lot. But they are sharper and more progressive and responsive than in the South. You don't just say salvation is by grace. They want to know why and how."

Rich is turned on to the renewal movement, though he "seldom mentions" government responsibilities in his sermons. "I stick to the moral and spiritual teaching of the Bible. I try to challenge everyone straight across the board." He says he encourages members to become involved in office prayer groups, and one Saturday morning each month his church has a prayer breakfast with key government leaders as speakers.

The McClean, Virginia, Bible Church flourishes in a more affluent suburb. Attendance is over twice the membership (175). Arizona Congressman John Conlan and his wife Irene attend because "it gives us what we want from the Bible." The Charles Colsons also attended after Mrs. Colson became involved in a neighborhood Bible study with women from the church. Julie Nixon Eisenhower, who was attracted to McClean through Bible studies at the Conlans, has also worshiped there.

Another independent evangelical congregation which attracts government people is the Barcroft Bible Church in Arlington, Virginia. The State Department's Cleo Shook is an elder and Sunday school teacher. Jan Ingersoll and Joyce

Adams from the White House staff along with Joyce's husband, Wayne, also attend.

Barcroft's pastor, C. Marlin "Butch" Hardman, says he has had his life and ministry "revolutionized by the training of lay people." He has "seen laymen win souls, follow them up, nurture them, counsel, administer, lead meetings, plant churches, train others, practice church discipline, minister to pastors".[1]

"Once I saw myself as a 'preacher' who ran here and there helping people, knowing that in the process something would happen," he recalls. "Now I see myself as an equipper of men for the work of service, and my pulpit teaching ministry has become even more meaningful." As a result, Hardman now evaluates his ministry "not in terms of meetings held, sermons preached, people counseled, offerings received, but in terms of lives developed for the work of the ministry."[2]

In 1973 the Barcroft church began quarterly elders' retreats. They go to a nearby motel for Friday evening and all day Saturday where, as the pastor notes: "[we] have time not only to deal with the issues but to get to know one another on a different level."[3]

Another effort to make Barcroft people "aware that members of the Body can minister to one another's needs" is a ten-to-fifteen-minute segment of evening services called "Body-Consciousness." During this time the pastor encourages members to intermingle, exchange name cards, and interact on some pertinent questions mentioned from the pulpit.

Getting to know people can be even more difficult in still larger churches such as National Presbyterian. This prestigious church dates from the time a group of Scottish stonemasons met for worship in a carpenter's shed on the White House grounds in 1793.

National Presbyterian recently relocated five miles from downtown Washington in the predominantly white northwest section of the city near the Maryland line. The massive stone-carved structure glitters with 60,000 pieces of colored glass in fifty-three windows, each of which portrays a biblical episode. It is owned and administered by the parent United Presbyterian denomination as a shrine and national center of conferences and special programs. The local congregation, in a sense, is merely permitted the use of the building for worship and Christian education.

The congregation over the years has included an impressive line of national leaders. The Chapel of the Presidents boasts pews once rented to Abraham Lincoln, Andrew Johnson, and fifteen other chief executives. The pre-dieu on which President Eisenhower knelt when baptized is on display.

The late J. Edgar Hoover, whose image of piety was marred after his death by disclosures that he kept juicy dossiers on certain government officials, taught Sunday school at National. The first funeral in the new sanctuary was held for Senate Minority Leader Everett McKinley Dirksen on September 10, 1969. Five pastors have been elected chaplains of the United States Senate.

With all its hallowed tradition, National Presbyterian—like many other urban churches across America—underwent a recession of sorts during the sixties and early seventies. Even after relocation few young couples were seen in worship services, and the Sunday school's high school class had only one teen-ager attending in early 1973. Following the retirement of senior minister Dr. Elson, the congregation summoned Dr. Louis Evans from a fashionable, fast-growing church in suburban San Diego, California, to take his place. (Elson continued in his duties as Senate chaplain.)

Soon after the arrival of the tall, handsome Evans and his wife Colleen, a former movie actress, National experienced a fresh infusion of life. Attendance picked up, interest in spiritual matters seemed high. In an interview during the period when Watergate was unraveling, Evans commented on what he saw: "Life is fast in southern California, but here there's a hustle and urgency among people who have the future of the world in their hands. Right now, perhaps because of Watergate, they are especially humble and reaching out for the Bible."

Evans says he is striving to bring National's people into a "covenant" relationship where they come to know Christ and each other on a deeper level. "My job," he adds, "is to call people to Christ and equip them to go into the community and touch Washington. If the Holy Spirit is alive and moving through their lives, then some beautiful changes can take place."

He and his wife promote "covenant groups" where participants role-play biblical characters, then "share their feelings in intimacy and honesty with fellow Christians who care." During the first nine-month period, nine made commitments, he reports. "This wasn't just a single evangelistic experience, but an entering into concern for one another. For instance, when one man had a very serious heart attack, two brothers in his covenant group did much more than go to the hospital and pray. They helped him sell his house and car, straightened out his insurance program, managed his estate, and parceled out his law practice to trusted colleagues."

Less than four miles farther north from National Presbyterian, just beyond the District line in well-to-do Bethesda, Maryland, is Fourth Presbyterian Church, a popular evangelical gathering spot. Fourth's pastor, Dr. Richard Halverson, a Princeton Seminary graduate, and Louis Evans are old friends. Halverson was a staff member at First Presbyterian Church in Hollywood, California, when Evans's father was senior minister there.

The white-haired, husky Halverson is more informal in the pulpit than Evans, who tends to take a more scholastic approach. A Bible expositor and exhorter, Halverson punches out short but meaning-laden sentences that the least educated in his congregation can understand. His warmth and enthusiasm have helped make Fourth's services at times seem more Baptist than Presbyterian.

He believes a local church should be "people centered rather than program centered" and "treat relationships between people and God and people as primary, ahead of program and work." He has tried to lead Fourth Church in becoming

a congregation that in itself would have all the elements of the small group—a congregation

> where the people would really love one another,
> where they would be conscious of their
> accountability to each other in the Lord, their
> priestly responsibilities, their responsibility to
> minister to one another as well as to the world
> outside. It would be a caring congregation, a loving
> congregation, a congregation that would literally
> demonstrate the reconciliation which it professed.[4]

To help worshipers "be aware of each other in more than a perfunctory, casual encounter," Halverson may ask them to link hands as they sing "Blest Be the Tie" and to turn and greet one another in an informal way, such as, "Good morning, it's a pleasure to be beside you. God bless you." Or to "pass the peace," an action where two assistant pastors say "The Peace of God Be with You" to persons sitting on the center-aisle end of each pew, who in turn pass it along their rows.

No personal kingdom builder, Halverson tells Fourth people that the "real work of the church is done between Sundays." If there's a conflict between a church organizational meeting and PTA, for example, he will encourage attendance at the latter. Numerical goals at church functions are not pushed. Yet throngs of Washingtonians of various political persuasions attend the three Sunday worship services at Fourth Presbyterian. Melvin Laird, Mark Hatfield, and John Anderson are regulars. During the heated debate over Viet Nam, evangelical satirist Joe Bayly quipped that at Fourth the "lion" (Laird) lies down with the "lamb" (Hatfield). Surprisingly, despite the presence of such nationally known government figures, Fourth is one of the least class-minded churches in Washington. Secretaries and clerks feel comfortable in the same pew with senators and judges.

Halverson does not like stewardship drives and preaches only one sermon a year on giving. But every Sunday he invites anyone in need to see one of the deacons during the coffee hour. The fifteen deacons are each given $50 at the beginning of a quarter to meet needs of persons they encounter. They are never required to report back on disbursements.

He promotes small weekday prayer and Bible study groups in houses and offices and ministry on a person-to-person basis. Several men from Fourth are involved in the "Man-to-Man" project where a volunteer commits himself to befriend a prison inmate, help him get a job when released, and provide personal contact as long as he wants it. Other laity are helping individuals with different needs. For example, Deacon James Cudney from the State Department counseled an ex-millionaire whose two children were in reform school and a distraught man whose father was mentally deranged.

Because Halverson embodies the servant concept of his deceased friend Abraham Vereide, he is probably the most welcomed Washington pastor in government offices. "When I walk into a senator's office," he says, "I don't want him or his staff thinking, 'Here comes Halverson; what does he want now?' I want them to be absolutely relaxed, knowing I have no axe to grind and want nothing except to be a blessing and to serve them in any way I can."

Comparing high government officials with entertainment figures in Hollywood where he once ministered, Halverson says, "The closer you get to the top the lonelier you are. People high up desperately need someone to love and care for them who does not seek to exploit them. A long time ago I saw that Jesus chose the twelve to be *with* Him. All his discipling rested on that word *with*. He established a relationship with the twelve and guided them in their relationships with each other. From that time I defined my ministry as being simply with men in order that they might be sent forth as witnesses of Jesus Christ."

Fourth Presbyterian Church and other suburban congregations do not face the challenges with which many inner-city Washington churches are confronted: racial change, flight of affluent white members, rising crime, and decaying housing. The D. C., population decreased slightly in the sixties (from 763,956 in 1960 to 756,510 in 1970), while the suburbs grew enormously from white newcomers and other whites moving further out. In the mid-seventies over 70 percent of D. C. population and over 95 percent of the public school enrollment was black.

During the period of rapid racial change many all-white D. C. churches either relocated or resigned themselves to inevitable decline. Less than thirty elderly whites now worship in one Baptist sanctuary seating 800. This church continues to draw a strong color line. The attractively designed downtown Westminister Presbyterian Church received only five new members in 1973 while losing twenty-six. With a membership of 132, only thirty-six were enrolled in Sunday school in mid-1974.

Rising crime has also contributed to the decline of historic downtown churches. Daytime attendance has fallen sharply and nighttime activities have been curtailed, especially since the incendiary riots that followed Martin Luther King's murder in 1968. Famed New York Avenue Presbyterian Church is down to 1,800 members from a high of 2,500. First Congregational United Church of Christ has dropped from 1,000 to less than five-hundred. National Baptist Memorial Church has fallen from 2,200 to below 1,000. After thirty major assaults on members and numerous thefts, National Baptist joined other downtown churches in locking doors and barring windows.

National Baptist is one of the best integrated inner-city churches. On an average Sunday there will be fifty international blacks, 100 local blacks, and 125 to 150 whites.

A more healthy downtown survivor is Foundry Methodist led by TV preacher Dr. Edward W. Bauman. The early morning free style service and the later traditional worship hour draw up to 1,600 each Sunday. There are prayer and study groups at five P.M. and a "healing" service at six. Church-sponsored social ministries include a preschool center for neighborhood children and a community counseling office. And Minister of Community Involvement James D. Palmer hopes the church can help "a thousand absolutely destitute elderly women who live within walking distance of the church."

The black Baptist churches are the strongest religious force in downtown Washington. The leading pastors control District politics. Mayor Walter Washington, a black, is an ordained minister as have been a majority of members on the D. C. Council.

A small group of these pastors influenced the D. C. Council of Churches to vote against official endorsement of a proposed Billy Graham Crusade. While conceding that individual congregations might wish to support the endeavor, the council declined on the basis that a Graham crusade would give only "religious legitimacy of the prevailing culture." The church, the council said, "exists to judge and help reshape the life style, structures, and values of the whole community." Graham's friendship with Richard Nixon did not help either. However, Graham backers—including several in Congress—still hope to bring the evangelist into D. C. for a major crusade.

The best publicized D. C. inner-city church is the unique Church of the Savior established by Southern Baptist army chaplain Gordon Cosby shortly after World War II. Tightly disciplined, the church's membership is only 114, with about 200 others participating. Besides weekly worship, a prospective member must commit himself to at least forty-five minutes of daily prayer and Bible study, contribute 10 percent of gross income, and participate in a group dedicated to a specific mission of change. Members must recommit themselves annually on the third Sunday in October.

Jerry Thompson, a middle management official in the Federal Energy Agency, is typical of many young government people attracted to the Church of the Savior because of its strong emphasis on building relationships within a group. "I attended a Baptist church back in Kansas for twenty years," he recalls, "and never knew how my closest friends in the congregation felt about the deeper things of life. In this church people are really concerned about loving God and one another. I feel free to express what I feel inside, not what I was told. I know what my relationship to Christ is and can talk to others about it."

The Church of the Savior is involved in a plethora of community service projects—including a farm, a coffee house (perhaps the first in the U.S.), community houses for the elderly, a church service agency which underwrites the cost of operating foster homes, and a special mission to congressmen called "Dunamis" after the Greek word for servant.

Six Dunamis groups seek to build personal relationships (both pastoral and prophetic) with key members of selected congressional committees. They prepare by spending from fifteen minutes to an hour a day in prayer and study about the personal background of committee members and issues on the committee agenda. Only after they feel empathy and understanding toward the targeted legislators do they begin calling on them to speak "prophetically" to the matter at hand. Even then they do not pressure a congressman to vote a certain way.

The Church of the Savior is not a typical church. It is more a ministry than an institution. It is more concerned for societal and individual needs than with building buildings and electing committees.

Richard Halverson feels that preoccupation with institutional structure is the Achilles heel of the big denominations. "I am not anti-institutional," he says, "but I think the big ecclesiastical monoliths have had their day. We are at the point now where the grass-roots are saying, 'Look, the vision begins here.' People are waking up to the fact that salvation is given to people, not a hierarchy."

In this regard it appears that the nondenominational evangelical groups are increasing in power and influence inside Washington even as many denominational churches are declining.

For example, the Christian Business Men's Committee has multiplied threefold within the last few years. CBMC members are taping radio spots aimed at local merchants, lobbyists, and other business representatives in Washington, setting up Bible classes, and correlating outreach with the independent Young Life and Campus Crusade for Christ organization. The charismatic Full Gospel Businessmen's group is pushing television outreach. They are in league with the Christian Broadcasting Network which has bought blocks of time on the local Channel 20.

At least three "house" ministries, somewhat like Fellowship House, have sprung up in recent years. Golfer Jim Hiskey manages Cornerstone House near the University of Maryland campus for students and young athletes. A counterpart for young career women is Trinity House near downtown Washington. Trinity was started by converted fashion model Windsor Elliot. Nearby Godfrey House began as a cafeteria and coffee house and now includes a bookstore and living quarters for guests.

There is less evangelical involvement with inner-city blacks, a matter which gives Bud Hancock "great concern." Hancock worked in Mayor Washington's office for two years—"the most important piece of education I ever received"—and saw "only token involvement of white evangelicals. The white liberals were trying," he recalls, "but their paternalism kept them from being well received."

Hancock and the mayor's black assistant, John Steiger, tried to bring rich, poor, black, and white together in a community prayer breakfast. They had only modest success and the breakfast has since been discontinued.

While counseling black youth in the Valley Green Housing Project, Hancock "realized that traditional evangelical programs were not effective in the ghetto structure." He saw that he "had to become involved in the family situation." Over a period of years he has tried to help one fatherless family that he found "enslaved to debt and alcohol. They are now all Christians and live in a better home. The mother has quit drinking and works regularly. One son is almost ready for college," he reports.

Kathryn Grant, Director of Baptist Women for the D. C. Baptist Convention, is another white leader concerned for the inner city. A former missionary to Japan, she came to her present post in 1971. One of her first actions was to escort a bus load of Baptist women, mostly from suburbs and many of them the wives of government workers, to "see Washington through Jesus' eyes." They talked with jail inmates, visited an orphan's home, stopped at Baptist mission centers, and concluded the evening with a walk along Thirteenth and Fourteenth Streets where pornography shops abound.

"These women had studied and given to foreign missions for years," Mrs. Grant notes. "They were shocked and appalled, and at every place found something positive to do."

Mrs. Grant's husband, Worth, is Washington representative for the Wycliffe Bible Translators. He teaches two large home Bible classes of Japanese women whose husbands work in Washington. "We spent twenty years in Japan," he says, "and never sensed such spiritual interest among Japanese. I think there we were regarded as paid American agents. Here they see us as friends from home who speak their language and understand their customs." He hopes that eventually a Japanese church may result from the Bible classes. Already there are Arabic, Chinese, Korean, Spanish, and other ethnic churches in Washington.

The cosmopolitan flavor of a city which has more than 120 foreign embassies is obvious. Diplomats and high-level employees of international agencies such as the Pan American Health Organization and the Organization of American States sit in conference rooms with their U. S. counterparts. Young men with foreign accents drive taxis. They are students from abroad working to help pay expenses at local colleges and universities. Some will return to become important leaders of their respective countries. "There are over 200,000 non-Americans in the Greater Washington area," Edward Davis, Management Liaison Specialist for the Organization of American States, estimates. Davis, Sunday school superintendent at Fourth Presbyterian, and son of a missionary to Mexico, has been with OAS twenty-five years. "Never embarrassed" at taking orange juice at receptions, Davis has helped set up OAS conferences throughout the hemisphere. Recently he assisted California Congressman Don Clausen in promoting a prayer luncheon for officials in Ecuador.

Davis and other key evangelicals in Washington-based international organizations have close ties with the Fellowship House. Here they bring foreign guests to hear Harold Hughes and other respected government figures give a Christian witness.

Three Fellowship House associates concentrate on

internationals. Pam Adams works local university campuses. Dick Hightower calls at embassies to build friendships, offer prayer and encouragement, and to help foreigners with the special problems they have in Washington. At opportune times he shares his faith. Each month Hightower coordinates a small prayer breakfast at Fellowship House for foreign ambassadors and evangelical congressmen. In the spring of 1974 he and Harold Hughes invited a number of United Nations delegates to a luncheon in New York. Among the thirteen who came were five Soviet diplomats. One asked Hughes why he was leaving the Senate. They listened intently as Hughes gave his Christian testimony. A second invited Hightower to be a house guest if he ever visits the Soviet Union.

Another Washington Christian who considers himself an "ambassador for Christ" in building friendships with foreigners is Lutheran layman Randy Stime. Ten years ago he was about to enroll in a Lutheran seminary when a friend introduced him to a Chinese colonel in California. "You Americans are stupid," the foreign officer said bluntly. "You spend millions sending AID people, Peace Corps workers, and missionaries overseas when you have future foreign leaders right in your own back yard. [The benefits of] all the dollars you spend are being undone by the inhospitality of Americans."

Stime borrowed $1,000 to make a survey of military bases where foreign officers were studying in the U. S. He discovered no hospitality program for them, either Christian or secular.

He presented his finding to friends in the Junior Chamber of Commerce. Their interest led to his coming to Washington and helping organize the International Jaycee Brotherhood Foundation for "building meaningful relationships" through hospitality for foreigners.

"The Foundation is not a mission," Stime cautions. "We are not arranging picnics, tours, and home visits with Christians per se, but with people who care and want to build friendships with foreigners. But we are finding that most of those who care are Christians."

Stime works through government and private agencies that relate to Washington-based foreigners. So does Minor Davidson, a former Baptist missionary to Indonesia who now serves under the Southern Baptist Home Mission Board. While Stime builds bridges between foreigners and individual Americans, Davidson tries to "get local churches to extend hospitality and friendship evangelism to foreigners."

"Superficially, Americans are the friendliest people in the world," Davidson notes. "But getting to know people from other cultures and religions takes a more extended relationship than a church meal or Sunday dinner in the home. Asians especially are misled by friendly hellos. They assume this will lead to deeper friendships and are shocked at the next meeting when Americans may not remember their names."

Davidson also calls at embassies. Last year he held a series of philosophical give-and-take debates with diplomats at Iron Curtain embassies. "Every embassy received us cordially except the Hungarians," he recalls. "We had two or three hours of free exchange at each place and found some diplomats to be quite knowledgeable of Christianity."

All of this is not the full story of what God is doing in Washington city and surrounding suburbs. It does indicate that there is more Christian witness and ministry going on in Washington than most American Christians have realized.

The challenge which Washington believers have accepted is to do more; to pray and work for a pervasive spiritual awakening in this the political nerve center of America and the diplomatic focal point of the world. They feel that what happens in Washington can spread spiritual and moral ripples around the globe.

CHAPTER TWELVE

Where to, America?

"O Lord our God, if ever we needed Thy wisdom and Thy guidance, it is now..."

So prayed Peter Marshall in his first appearance as chaplain of the United States Senate. The date was January 6, 1947. The euphoria and relief felt over victory in World War II was vanishing while fears of nuclear war between Russia and the United States were increasing.

The worries *then* were big *then*, but today they seem miniscule in comparison. Hardly anyone disputes the contention that America is in deep, deep trouble. After coming out of Watergate, the nation is plagued by the twin economic maladies of inflation and recession, while keeping a nervous eye on the volatile Middle East and other foreign threats to the precarious peace.

"Americans are like Jonathan Livingston Seagull," Dr. Herbert Eber of Atlanta told a March 1974 conference of Georgia psychologists. "We are in a holding pattern, looking for a place to land ... sometimes wishing we could go back to where we took off from, but there's nothing to go back to.

"Our world is falling apart. We all feel so frustrated. Our power has grown faster than our ability to manage it."

Journalist Bill Moyers, press secretary for President Lyndon Johnson and before that a Baptist theological student, thinks American democracy is undergoing its greatest trial since the Civil War. "Americans are like a huddled group of sheep,

187

waiting for a political Messiah," he says.

Such warnings have become commonplace and fall on public senses dulled by televised violence, both imagined and real. Many who do listen shrug and say that doomsayers have always been with us. America is resilent, they say, and has always come back after every crisis. To some degree this is happening in reference to Watergate.

Congress is moving to right the balance between the executive and legislative branches of government that had been tipping toward the White House since Roosevelt's New Deal. A new bill makes Congress a partner with the White House in drawing up the Federal budget.

Congress has tightened the laws on political campaign financing. It is hoped this will close the door to illegal and secret contributions.

Several states have enacted major political reforms.

In 1974 California voters passed one of the strictest laws on political reform ever written. Regulations on lobbyists are tightened. Campaign contributions over $50 must be reported. All state and local officials whose financial interests could be bettered by their own decisions are required to file annual financial statements.

A new Alabama code forbids top officeholders from holding financial interest in any enterprise doing business with the State.

Ten states have passed "Sunshine Laws," opening all meetings of governmental bodies to citizen attendance.

The American Bar Association now requires every law school in the country to teach courses in ethics. Lawyers seeking admission to the bar in California must answer questions on ethics. (Most of those charged with Watergate crimes were lawyers.)

Politics is a major topic of conversation on campuses. Law schools have more applicants than can be admitted.

Christian schools are stepping up programs on politics and public affairs. For example, Calvin College's "Washington Project," under political science professor Dr. Paul Henry, allows students to work in congressional offices for academic credit. Calvin College also holds an annual conference on

Christianity and politics.

Ouachita Baptist University, a small Arkansas school has established an ambitious Public Affairs Center that will:

—Establish a permanent public opinion research program involving faculty and students and seminars for high school civics teachers and selected students.

—Bring speakers to the campus to help dispel negative images of politics and public service.

—Take selected groups of students to different centers of important political activity to observe firsthand the workings of the political process.

—Organize mid-winter comparative government study tours to selected foreign capitals.

Ouachita's president, Dr. Daniel R. Grant, formerly taught political science at Vanderbilt. He believes "one of the greatest tragedies that could grow out of this crisis (Watergate) would be for American young people to decide that politics and public service are hopelessly corrupt, that the only way to obtain and hold high public office is through illegitimate means, and that no self-respecting young person should commit his life to a career in government and politics.

"There has probably never been a greater need in our nation's history for a creative demonstration on ... campus of a way to combine both the realism and the idealism of the political process in the education of our young people."

The most significant recent happening in education may be the establishment of the new International Law School by Christians in Washington. The school was proposed at a Friday prayer luncheon in the Federal Bar Association building by Phil W. Jordan, former assistant director of the Secret Service. A board of trustees was formed, a faculty with unquestioned moral standards secured, and Dr. John Brabner-Smith, a former crimebusting lawyer in the Justice Department and a regular at the Friday prayer luncheon, elected the first president.

"After Phil presented the idea," Brabner-Smith recalls, "we made a study and found that other law schools were not stressing the moral absolutes revealed in the Bible and on which the American system of law and government was founded. We also discovered that many schools were basing their admission policy almost entirely on test scores, with little reference to the motivation, character, and maturity of students. This astounded us, because no profession tests one's personal morality and integrity more than law."

The faculty of the new school is biblically grounded and subscribes to a tight code of ethics, Brabner-Smith says. For example, Dr. John Warwick Montgomery, who formerly taught at Trinity Evangelical Divinity School, teaches biblical jurisprudence. "Historically," Brabner-Smith points out, "the great teachers of jurisprudence—the foundations of morality upon which law rests—were theologians. We feel that the American educational system, particularly law schools, must return to teaching foundational truth. A pluralistic society like the United States cannot continue free without a shared morality. It will dissolve or be taken over by force."

All well and good. But America may not be able to afford the time it takes for idealistic students to get into the political process. What of the great masses of Americans beyond college age?

The commentary of returning Viet Nam POW Colonel Norris M. Overly is worth noting. He senses a "certain malaise in the air, a frustration of bigness in government, universities, and industry, a conviction that the individual is being ground down before the onslaught of civilization, an inclination to escape, retreat to the simple life, to be self-centered and let someone else shoulder the load—to drop out, cop out."

There is plenty of evidence that this is happening. For example, only 38 percent of voting age Americans even bothered to vote in the 1974 congressional elections. And according to editors of *U.S. News and World Report Books* 97 percent of Americans are not active in politics beyond voting.

> They give nothing to any political party—no money, no work at the polls, no attendance at precinct meetings, no service as a volunteer worker for any candidate. They sit back, allowing others to get the job done. This leaves the running of

government in the hands of 3 percent of the American people.[1]

Furthermore, Gallup polls have found that 57 percent of Americans cannot name their Congressman and 81 percent cannot cite a single thing he has done. Ralph Nader says Americans know far more about entertainers and football players than about their elected representatives.

Sad to say, such apathy and ignorance appears to be endemic among American evangelical Christians, whose forerunners (Roger Williams, Thomas Hooker, and William Penn, for example) were among the leading shapers of the American system. To illustrate: A survey of voting habits in Chicago during a recent four-year period showed that only 17 percent of the Protestant ministers even bothered to go to the polls, while 99 percent of the tavern-keepers cast ballots.

Walter Fauntroy, the D. C. delegate to Congress who is also a Baptist pastor, suggests one solution: "We've got to educate the masses of Christians that they are to be *in the world* serving God, but not *of the world. In the world* includes being active in political life. *Of the world* involves corruption and dishonesty. The Lord needs workers from the precinct level up. We either get into the process or leave it to the devil."

"The Lord's command to 'go into all the world' is vocational as well as geographic," says conservative Republican John Conlan. "We Bible-believing Christians have been asleep at the switch, thinking Christian influence of the past carries on to this generation. 'Let George do it' is the cancer among us that must be cured."

Conlan believes Bible prophecy teaches the world will get steadily worse until Christ returns. "Until then," he says, "we are responsible to get Christians into office. We've misinterpreted Paul's command to 'come out from among them and be separate' to mean 'eat meat and retreat.' " He further laments that "we evangelicals have been sending our best young people to Africa, Latin America, and Asia as missionaries, while socialists and humanists have been sending their best into politics, education, and communications here at home."

Jack Buttram, the veteran campaign aide and lobbyist, would like political candidates selected the way deacons and elders are chosen in churches. "Because we think those jobs are important we look around and see who is the best qualified. Why don't we put our hand on Christians we think should be in politics, ask them to run, and if they consent, help them get elected?"

Professors Robert D. Linder and Richard V. Pierard (in their incisive *Politics: A Case for Christian Action*) believe that evangelical Christians can make "distinctive contributions" in politics by:

1. Influencing the middle majority of voters. Followers of Christ are in a better position to do this than extremists because they "understand the need for balance and moderation."

2. Showing "from the Scripture that the humanistic, utopian dream of a better society constructed by the hand of man alone is a false hope." By knowing man's "potential for evil," Linder and Pierard say, "Christians are protected from falling into either the left-wing trap of idealizing the dispossessed and downtrodden or the right-wing snare of confusing material benefits with spiritual well-being."

3. Following "a social conscience based upon the Word of God" in which they pursue the "divine commands to love their neighbor and seek his welfare."

4. "Bringing to the political realm a sense of integrity that so often is lacking there." Christians "recognize that certain absolutes underlie human society and that their lives must be brought into conformity with these absolutes."

5. Using political power as an implement of the stewardship which God has given Christians over his creation.[2]

But will politics alone be sufficient to solve the grave problems which confront us? The prestigious *London Times* suggests, for example, that inflation cannot be cured by politicians. It is a "religious and moral problem," says the *Times,* to be remedied, if at all, "by priests and preachers and prophets and moralists. At best politicians and parliaments can mitigate the damage; they can't go to the root of the problem.

"What is inflation, after all?" the *Times* asks. "It's an economist's word for overconsumption; for living beyond your income; for taking more out of the kitty than you put in... Overlooking these realities,... we have built into the structures of our society the deadly sins of pride, envy, avarice, gluttony, and sloth... Capital, management, labor, they all depend upon our continued addiction to levels of consumption which cannot possibly be sustained. Those five deadly sins are their bread and butter, and therefore inflamed by every advertising campaign, every trade union campaign."

This leaves us only our churches, the *Times* concludes. "If they cannot, or cannot be bothered (to help us), we are in a bad way indeed."[3]

Addressing himself to American Christians on the problem of world hunger—which has worsened because of inflation, Mark Hatfield asks:

> What is our life style? Is it characterized by consumption or by conservation? What determines our needs—the television, magazines, friends, cultures? What determines our buying patterns today? More gadgets, the best, most colorful, the easiest to care for? Are the determining factors the throw-away ethic, convenience and disposability? We as Christians have the first obligation to review our life styles.[4]

John F. Alexander, editor of *The Other Side* and a leading voice from the socially active "new evangelicals," calls for Christians to adopt "a politics of love. Love dictates the goals in politics, but it does not dictate the means (at least not as clearly)," he says. "The best means are found by hardheaded analysis and experimentation, not by appeal to revelation. If a person is a Christian he will know he should be concerned about high unemployment, but he won't automatically know whether unemployment can best be decreased by tax cuts, government construction projects, or unbridled competition in an open market....[5]

Alexander thinks the "hard thing" is not finding the means,

but commitment to the goal of loving help for others. We would find ways to our goals if we were really committed to them, he believes. "The present welfare system has not been astonishingly unsuccessful, but if Americans wanted to solve this problem we would experiment until we found a way that would work. What we lack is not the means to end poverty but the desire to end it. If we accepted the goal of ending racial discrimination, we could do it—but we won't. And the reason is not that we lack the means. The reason is that we have not accepted the goal which Christ has given us."[6]

Louis Evans sees encouraging signs that more people are coming to this commitment. "There's a rising third party in the church replacing the old dictum where you were either a soul saver or a social worker." In this new party, Evans says, "you meet Christ and go out in the world to change what needs changing, correct oppression, clothe the naked, pursue peace, and do all that the gospel says we should have been doing all along. It is a balanced ministry to the spiritual, social, economic, and political person."

There are encouraging indications that this is beginning to happen among evangelicals. Take only two examples:

The First Baptist Church of Pensacola, Florida, recently obtained $50,000 in city money and recruited volunteers to refurbish 100 homes in poverty areas. This church has been so involved in the community that "when the city government is starting anything, they contact the church to see how we can get involved," Pastor James Pleitz says.

Chicago's LaSalle Street Church, a much smaller congregation with only 125 members, operates a legal aid bureau for inner-city poor, a counseling center with a sliding scale of payment so all can afford help, a skill-building program for high-school dropouts, and is helping to build a housing project with the help of federal funds for moderate income families who otherwise could not find decent housing.

In ways like this a Christian can "be more patriotic than his unbelieving neighbor," Dr. Robert Mounce, professor of religious studies at Western Kentucky University, thinks. This, he contends, is because the Christian "is committed to the truth, to justice, and self-sacrifice. Having been redeemed by Christ and empowered by the Spirit, should he not play a leading role in setting the standard of true patriotism?"[7]

Rep. John Anderson holds that the "new evangelical majority in American religion bears a heavy responsibility for the nation's future." In April 1974 he told delegates at the National Association of Evangelicals convention in Boston that evangelicals had replaced theological liberals as the "in" group among Washington leaders. Recalling the days of Franklin D. Roosevelt when liberal churchmen were hailing federal social programs for helping to bring in the kingdom, Anderson declared:

> It was *they* (the liberals) who denied the supernatural acts of God, conforming the gospel to the canons of modern science. It was *they* who advocated laws and legislation as the modern substitutionary atonement for the sins of mankind. It was *they* who found financial support for architectural monuments to their cause. It was *they* who were the friends of those in positions of political power. *They* were the "beautiful people", and *we*—you will recall—were the "kooks." We were regarded as rural, reactionary, illiterate fundamentalists who just didn't know better.
>
> Well, things have changed. Now *they* are the "kooks"—and *we* are the "beautiful people." *Our* prayer breakfasts are so popular that only those with engraved invitations are allowed to attend. *Our* evangelists have the ready ear of those in positions of highest authority. *Our* churches are growing, and theirs are withering... *They* are tired, worn-out 19th century liberals trying to repair the pieces of an optimism shattered by world wars, race riots, population explosion, and the spectre of worldwide famine. *We* always knew that things would get worse before the Lord came again.

Anderson warned that "the very success of the evangelical movement in recent years" could "threaten to be its undoing."

We suddenly find ourselves as the "comfortable" ones in American society today. What are we to do with our comfort? Are we to bathe ourselves in it, or to use it to salve the wounds of those who are suffering? Are we going to close our eyes to the world around us, or are we going to keep them open so that we may teach others to see as well? Are we going to jealously protect our wealth, or are we going to sell what we have to give to the poor?

These are searching questions that call for thoughtful answers from Christians concerned about the emerging third century of the world's oldest democracy. Washington Christians may have pointed the way in fulfilling the spirit of Peter Marshall's last prayer written for the U. S. Senate in 1949:

Deliver us, our Father, from futile hopes and from clinging to lost causes, that we may move into ever-growing calm and ever-widening horizons.

Where we cannot convince, let us be willing to persuade, for small deeds done are better than great deeds planned.

We know that we cannot do everything. But help us to do something. For Jesus' sake. *Amen.*

Authors' Note

We could not have written this book without the cooperation of scores of Capitol Christians, many of them in
government—from United States senators to employees in
the lowest echelons of the federal bureaucracy. Although
each one contributed valuable substance to our reservoir of
information, space limitation and the need to avoid undue
repetition prevented us from quoting or citing as examples
everyone with whom we spoke. But we are grateful to them
all for taking time from busy schedules to reflect on their
experiences and to offer observations, enabling us to get a
better view of the variegated Washington scene.

We conducted our interviews in a period when reporters
were being hailed by some as sainted benefactors of society
and vilified as vultures by others. Thus we were
impressed—and relieved—by the warmly open yet no-halo
reception our story subjects gave us when we called. We were
also impressed by their willingness to level freely with us
about tensions as well as brighter aspects of their personal
and vocational lives.

On our part, we have sought to safeguard as much as
possible their privacy in spiritual matters, to avoid character
glamorization, and to portray accurately their personalities
and views though admittedly within very limited contexts.
Our central purpose has been simply to chronicle a
remarkable God-centered movement portending good news
in an important time and locale saturated with bad news.

Among persons of special help were Kathryn Grant, a Baptist lay leader; Barbara Priddy, a Christian worker; Lt. Commander Stephen R. Harris of *Pueblo* fame; and consultant-missionary Robert L. "Bud" Hancock. They pointed out many persons we might otherwise have missed. Fellow newsmen Jack Novotney, Washington correspondent for Religious News Service, and Wesley Pippert, who covers Congress for United Press International (he was UPI's chief Watergate reporter), provided valuable background information. Pastor Richard Halverson of suburban Washington's Fourth Presbyterian Church and Douglas Coe, a full-time lay worker, reviewed and offered suggestions on the chapter about Abraham Vereide and International Christian Leadership.

The Washington office of the Summer Institute of Linguistics lent a desk and telephone during the period of research.

Our wives, Marti Hefley and Rose Plowman, were patient and hospitable when we worked together on crash schedules at our respective homes. Marti did most of the interviews for the chapter on women in Washington. Rose did some of the final typing of the manuscript.

Most of the secretarial work—transcribing about sixty hours of taped interviews and typing much of the manuscript—was done by Nancy Gillam.

Finally, we are grateful to the publishers who gave permission for use of copyrighted material that served to supplement a number of interviews. Appropriate credits are given in the bibliographical notes.

James C. Hefley
Edward E. Plowman

References

CHAPTER TWO
1. C. S. Lewis, *Mere Christianity,* copyright Macmillan Publishing Co., Inc., 1964, p. 109. Used by permission.
2. *Harper's Magazine,* October, 1973.

CHAPTER THREE
1. *New York Times,* January 31, 1974.

CHAPTER FOUR
1. March 24, 1974.
2. Unpublished "Link Service Manual," p. 5.

CHAPTER SIX
1. From a speech given in 1969 and later printed in Hatfield's *Conflict and Conscience,* copyright, Word, Inc., Waco, Texas, 1971, pp. 112-14. Used by permission.
2. *Conflict and Conscience,* p. 13.
3. Ibid, pp. 162-3.
4. Ibid, p. 165.

CHAPTER SEVEN
1. Syndicated column, May 24, 1974.
2. 2 Corinthians 5:17, 18, *Phillips.*

CHAPTER EIGHT
1. *Los Angeles Times,* April 25, 1974.
2. From "Church and State in America," copyright 1970 by Albert H. Quie and appearing in *Congress and Conscience,* edited by John B. Anderson and published by J. B. Lippincott Company, Philadelphia and New York, 1970, p. 150. Used by permission.
3. Ibid, p. 123.
4. February 17, 1974.
5. Excerpted from "The Just God Judges the Nations," an address delivered by Congressman John B. Anderson to the National Association of Evangelicals meeting in Boston, April 22-26, 1974.

CHAPTER TEN

1. *Laughing All the Way,* Fawcett Crest edition reprinted by arrangement with Stein and Day, Incorporated, 1973, p. 99.
2. May, 1974, p. 140.
3. "Joan Kennedy: Woman Under Pressure," *Ladies Home Journal,* September, 1974, p. 60.

CHAPTER ELEVEN

1. *Christianity Today,* July 26, 1974, p. 27.
2. Ibid, August 30, 1974, p. 23.
3. Ibid.
4. Richard C. Halverson, *How I Changed My Thinking About the Church,* copyright Zondervan Publishing House, Grand Rapids, 1972, p. 16. Used by permission.

CHAPTER TWELVE

1. "U.S. Politics—Inside and Out," copyright 1970, U. S. News & World Report, Inc., Washington, D.C. 20037, p. 78.
2. Taken from *Politics: A Case for Christian Action* by Linder and Pierard. Copyright 1973 by Inter-Varsity Christian Fellowship and used by permission of Inter-Varsity Press.
3. Quotations noted in *The Alliance Witness,* official publication of the Christian & Missionary Alliance, Nyack, New York, January 29, 1975.
4. *World Vision,* article entitled "World Hunger: More Explosive Than Atomic Weaponry," pp. 6, 7.
5. Reprinted from an editorial by John F. Alexander, *The Other Side,* July-August, 1972, p. 2.
6. Ibid, p. 3.
7. *Applied Christianity,* April, 1974, p. 17.